INTRODUCTORY PSYCHOLOGY SERIES

DEVELOPMENTAL PSYCHOLOGY:

FROM INFANCY TO ADULTHOOD

By Ann Birch and Tony Malim

ISSN 0953-1564   ISBN: 1-871010-00-4

Published by Intertext Limited
Equity & Law Building
30-34 Baldwin Street, Bristol BS1 1NR

Cartoons by Sally Artz
Typesetting by Avonset, Midsomer Norton, Bath
Designed and produced by Colourways, Clevedon, Bristol

CONTENTS

ABOUT THE AUTHORS

Ann Birch has a Masters Degree in Education with specialization in psychology from Bristol University and is a member of the British Psychological Society. She has taught psychology at A and O/A levels for seven years and currently lectures in psychology and teacher education at Weston-super-Mare College of Further Education and is a visiting lecturer at Bristol Polytechnic. She is an assistant examiner of O/A level psychology.

Tony Malim has a first degree from Cambridge in classics and history and a Masters Degree in Education with specialization in psychology from Lancaster University. He has taught A level psychology virtually from its inception as a pilot project in 1972 and has been an assistant examiner in the subject. His present post is that of Head of the School of Social Sciences at Weston-super-Mare College of Further Education.

INTRODUCTION

This is the first in a series of short books providing comprehensive notes suitable for students of A level or first-year degree level Psychology. It includes discussion of relevant theory, up-to-date research evidence and practical applications of psychological knowledge. The books in this series can be used for private study or as supplementary material and exercises to accompany a taught course. Each chapter includes self-assessment questions and recommended further reading.

To obtain a sound grasp of developmental psychology, the reader is advised to work through the text a section at a time and to consider the self-assessment questions at the end of each section. The self-assessment questions might then be re-considered after further reading has been undertaken.

Ann Birch

Tony Malim

"I TRIED OBSERVATIONAL TECHNIQUES — WAS JUST ABOUT TO MOVE INTO INTERVIEWS..."

Chapter 1

Research Methods in Developmental Psychology

At the end of this chapter you should be able to:

1   describe a range of research designs and methods used in developmental psychology;

2   discuss the strengths and limitations of each design or method.

Developmental psychology is the study of the psychological changes that take place between birth and old age. Most research has focused upon childhood and adolescence. The study of adults did not emerge to any great extent until after the second world war. Even today there are relatively few psychologists who study adulthood, and only the study of the aged has received substantial attention from researchers.

In order to study human behaviour scientifically, developmental psychologists use a number of different research designs and methods: those most commonly used are summarised below.

A   RESEARCH DESIGNS

Where the aim is to observe age-related changes in some area of psychological functioning, two principal designs are used to gather information about individuals at different points in their development: cross-sectional and longitudinal.

1   Cross-sectional design

Groups of individuals of different ages are compared at the same point of time. For example, researchers who wish to compare moral values held during early adulthood with those held during middle-age will make observations or carry out tests on groups of both young and middle aged adults at one time. Conclusions will then be drawn about moral values at these two age levels.

Strengths

(a)   It is quick and relatively inexpensive.

(b)   It can be easily replicated.

(c)   It can identify differences between age groups and general trends in development which may then be studied more intensively.

Limitations

(a)   Because behaviour is observed at only one time, it tells us nothing about development within individuals.

(b)   People of widely differing age groups will have received different social and cultural experiences. Results may reflect these differences rather than differences due to age.

2   **Longitudinal Design**

One group of individuals will be studied over a period of time, usually a number of years. Observations and tests will be carried out at various time intervals. Thus, a study of moral values during adulthood might involve testing one group of adults every 10 years between the ages of 20 and 60.

Strengths

(a)   It provides a view of the development of individuals over time.

(b)   Questions can be answered about the stability of behaviour.

(c)   It may be possible to determine the effects of earlier experience and conditions on later development.

Limitations

(a)   It requires a large investment of time and money.

(b)   Subjects may be lost or drop out. Those who remain may form a biased group.

(c)   Replication may not be realistic because of changes in societal influences at different points in time.

B   **METHODS OF STUDY**

1   **Experiments**
Manipulation and control are key features of the experimental

method. The investigator **manipulates** one variable — called the **independent variable** — and observes its effect on another variable — called the **dependent variable**. At the same time, all other factors which might affect the dependent variable are controlled. Experiments are usually carried out in a laboratory, though they may take place in a more natural setting.

The study by Bandura, Ross and Ross (1963) described on page 64 is an example of a strictly controlled laboratory experiment. The aim was to investigate how far models influence aggressive behaviour in children. Exposure to an aggressive model was the independent variable and the number of aggressive acts reproduced by the children was the dependent variable.

Strengths

(a) Because unwanted variables are strictly controlled, it is possible to draw firm conclusions about whether the independent variable affected the dependent variable, that is, whether there was a **cause-effect** relationship between the two.

(b) Experiments provide precise and objective information about human behaviour. Because of this precision, they can usually be easily **replicated**.

Limitations

(a) Most experiments are short term. One therefore cannot be sure that the behaviour observed would be the same in the longer term 'real world' situation.

(b) Subjects observed under relatively restricted laboratory conditions may not behave as they would in a more natural setting.

(c) Some kinds of behaviour cannot be experimentally manipulated. For example, children cannot be deliberately exposed to deprivation or abuse in order to examine the effects on their development.

2   Observational techniques

The natural behaviour of individuals is observed and recorded with as little intervention from the observer as possible. The following two main observational techniques are used.

(i) Naturalistic observation

Spontaneous, ongoing behaviour is observed in a natural setting. An example is the study of children's play activities by Sylva *et al.* (1980) described on page 22.

Strength

Observational techniques give a more realistic picture of how people function in their everyday world.

Limitations

(a) Because of the lack of strict control, it is not possible to be sure whether or not unwanted variables are affecting the behaviour studied. One cannot therefore infer cause and effect relationships.

(b) Observational techniques are more open to potential observer bias than are other methods, since they rely more heavily upon the observer's subjective interpretation of events.

(ii) Controlled observation

Spontaneous behaviour is observed, but in a situation which has to some extent been manipulated and controlled by the observer.

Ainsworth's studies of infants' reactions to a strange situation referred to on page 8 are examples of controlled observation (Ainsworth & Wittig 1969). Typically, a mother and infant interact in an observation room equipped with a one-way mirror. The babies' reactions to different events are recorded by the investigator. For example, the mother may leave the room or a stranger may approach either during the mother's presence or when she has left the room.

Strengths

(a) This method has much in common with naturalistic observation, with its emphasis on observing spontaneous behaviour.

(b) Since the environment in which the behaviour occurs has to some extent been controlled, the investigator can be more confident about which variables are influencing subjects' behaviour.

Limitation

As the setting in which the observations are made are often unfamiliar to the subjects, the behaviour observed may not be typical of that which would occur in a more natural setting.

3 Interview techniques

These usually involve one-to-one interchanges between the investigator and the subjects. Initially questions may be asked in a relatively standard way. Subsequent questions may vary in the light of subjects' answers/

Piaget's **clinical interview** method is one example of this technique. (See Chapter 3.)

Strength

It is a flexible and effective means of gaining a detailed picture of a person's thought processes, attitudes, fantasies, etc. which are not usually available for direct observation.

Limitations

(a) The lack of standardisation results in questions varying slightly from one person to another. The interviewer may 'lead' the subject to views she/he does not possess.

(b) The reliance placed on language as a means of communication limits this method to subjects whose own understanding and use of language is well-developed. It may not, therefore, be a suitable method to use with young children or retarded people.

4 Correlation

This statistical technique is used in many studies to discover whether or not there is a relationship between two variables/For example, Huesmann (1982) recorded the amount of violent TV watched by a group of primary schoolchildren. The level of aggressive behaviour displayed by the children at school was also recorded. The investigators then correlated the data to determine whether those children who watched the most violence on TV also displayed the most aggressive behaviour. Findings revealed a positive correlation between the two variables.

Strength

This technique allows an investigator to measure relationships between naturally occurring variables, without manipulating or controlling them.

Limitations

The use of correlation does not permit an investigator to draw conclusions about **cause and effect**. Some other factor, unknown to the investigator, may be responsible for the findings. For example, children who display highly aggressive behaviour may have an innate pre-disposition to behave aggressively, which in turn may motivate them to watch more violent TV programmes.

WHICH METHOD?

All the methods described have both strengths and weaknesses. The method chosen by an investigator will depend largely upon the aspect of development being studied.

Ideally, a number of different methods should be used within one study. If these different methods produce similar findings, confidence can be placed in the conclusions drawn.

SELF-ASSESSMENT QUESTIONS

1   Which research design, cross-sectional or longitudinal, do you consider the most appropriate for the study of children's patterns of play behaviour at different ages? Give reasons for your answer.

2   Evaluate the usefulness of experimental methods in developmental psychology compared with other approaches?

3   Consider some of the factors which might influence an investigator's choice of research method.

FURTHER READING

Bee H **The developing child** (4th Edition). New York Harper & Row 1985.

Gardner H **Developmental psychology**. Boston, Toronto Little, Brown & Co. 1982.

McGurk H **Growing and changing**. Methuen 1975.

Mussen P, J J Conger, & J Kagan **Child development and personality** (6th Edition) New York Harper 1984.

Chapter 2

Early Socialisation

At the end of this chapter you should be able to:

1   understand the concept of socialisation;

2   describe some of the major milestones in social and emotional development in infants, in particular the phenomenon of attachment;

3   describe the views of Bowlby and other researchers concerning the nature and significance of attachment;

4   discuss the implications for human development of
   —   deprivation in monkeys,
   —   studies of animal imprinting;

5   Assess critically Bowlby's views on maternal deprivation in the light of subsequent re-assessments of his work;

6   Assess the importance of early experience for later social and emotional development, in the light of the available evidence;

7   discuss the nature and functions of play in early childhood.

SECTION I: THE DEVELOPMENT OF ATTACHMENT

SOCIALISATION

Socialisation is a concept which is used to describe and explain how children acquire the behaviour necessary to enable them to fit in with their culture or society. One definition is: the process by which someone learns the ways of a given society, or social group, so that he/she can function within it.

In infancy, the socialisation process is influenced most by the parents, who act as models for acceptable behaviour, provide loving support and decide on which behaviours to restrict and which to allow.

In psychology, the concept of socialisation encompasses more than the learning process involved in development; it also endeavours to take account of the part played by the genetic potential of the individual in responding to the influences upon her/him.

7

While the term socialisation used to be applied exclusively to the developing behaviour of the child, it has over the past few years widened to consider the adjustments and changes which take place through life. This chapter, however, will be concerned with some of the processes which influence social and emotional development in infants and younger children, and will consider in particular the development and significance of intimate attachments which form between a child and the adults who care for her or him.

MILESTONES IN SOCIAL AND EMOTIONAL DEVELOPMENT

Social smiling

A necessary precursor to the socialisation process is the existence of communication, or 'social signals', between child and adults. One such signal which has been investigated is social smiling.

Voluntary smiling (that is, smiling which occurs in response to overtures from an adult) usually occurs when the infant is around four to six weeks old. Smiles are initially elicited by a variety of stimuli, including faces, bells, and bullseyes, but gradually they are reserved for social contexts, with the human face being the most likely stimulus to encourage smiles. From the second and third months the child seems capable of recognising particular faces and thereafter is most likely to smile in response to familiar people, such as members of the family or regular visitors. Less familiar individuals will elicit only weak smiles. Infant smiles appear to serve as a powerful mechanism which is designed to attract the attention and proximity of adults.

Stranger anxiety

At about the age of eight to nine months, a child will exhibit what Spitz has described as 'eight months' anxiety'. This refers to the wariness or open distress which the young child displays when presented with a strange adult. The phenomenon of 'stranger anxiety' has been studied by Ainsworth (1969, 1974).

Attachment

A young child's tendency to seek closeness to certain people and to feel secure when they are present is known as attachment.

Bowlby (1969) believes there are several stages in the development of attachment. Initially, the child is universally sociable, not caring who responds to its overtures. Once it is able to discriminate among individuals it begins to demonstrate preferences which become more marked over the following few months. The first strong attachments appear to form around seven to eight months. Once the baby is mobile,

8

attachment behaviour includes moving towards, staying close, separation protest, clinging and using the adult as a 'secure base' from which to explore. These behaviours are, Bowlby believes, designed to encourage physical (and later, psychological) closeness to the mother.

Ainsworth (1974) proposed that the quality of the attachment formed between the child and mother depends upon the mother's sensitivity to the child's emotional needs. Most babies experience '**secure attachment**'; some, whose mothers have responded less readily to their needs, develop '**anxious attachment**'.

Schaffer (1977) drew attention to the '**mutual reciprocity**' of the infant-mother relationship. He describes the sensitive and finely balanced patterns of interaction which occur as each responds to the activities of the other and each influences the behaviour of the other. The strength of the attachment formed does not appear to be related to the basic care given in relation to feeding, dressing, etc, or to the amount of interaction, but more to the quality and sensitivity of the adult's responsiveness to the infant's signals.

For the majority of infants, the object of their attachment is initially the mother. Bowlby and other researchers believe that the attachment bond which forms between an infant and its mother forms the basis of all interpersonal relationships in later years. More recent research has stressed the importance of attachments which form with other adults, particularly the father.

Psychologists have been interested in the phenomenon of attachment from a number of points of view, and have posed several complex questions in the course of their research. Among these are the following.

1   Does the mother-child bond occur because the mother feeds and protects the child, or does it depend also on such factors as the provision of love and stimulation?

2   Must the child's mother be involved in the initial bonding, or could the attachment be formed with the father, or even with a group of other adults?

3   What are the consequences, if any, for later social and emotional development if a bond does not form?

MATERNAL DEPRIVATION

Interest in the last question was prompted in the 1940s and 1950s by evidence concerning the effects of institutionalisation on social and emotional development. Children who had grown up in institutions frequently seemed to display listlessness and troubled behaviour, and showed no interest in social interaction (Bowlby 1951).

Two main sources provided information:

9

1   the animal studies carried out by Harlow and associates into the effects of maternal deprivation on infant monkeys, and by Lorenz into imprinting behaviour in creatures such as ducks and geese;

2   John Bowlby's studies of maternal deprivation in human infants.

Harlow's studies of deprivation in monkeys

The traditional view of the mother-child relationship held by psychologists who subscribe to environmental-learning theory is that attachments are formed as a result of need-gratification. The mother, as a source of food, satisfies the child's basic physiological needs. Harlow (1958), a prominent investigator of animal behaviour in the USA, put this supposition to the test in a series of controlled experiments carried out with rhesus monkeys over a period of some 20 years. Harlow's experiments took several forms.

(a) Infant monkeys were removed from their mothers shortly after birth and were placed alone in a cage with a surrogate (or substitute) mother. The surrogate mothers were of two kinds: either a 'cloth mother' which consisted of a cylinder of wood covered with soft, terry-towelling material, or a 'wire mother', which was simply a wire cylinder. Both were of the same size and general shape as an adult monkey. Each 'mother' was equipped with a feeding bottle so that the infant could nurse from it. Each monkey had the opportunity to gain access to the other surrogate mother.

The revolutionary finding was that, irrespective of which 'mother' provided the nourishment, each infant spent most of its time clinging to the cloth mother. Harlow concluded that baby primates need a source of warmth, or '**contact comfort**', in addition to the source of food.

When, during a follow-up experiment, the monkeys were deliberately frightened by the appearance of a 'bear monster' in the form of a wind-up toy, those infants raised exclusively by the cloth mother raced and clung to their 'mother', while those reared by the wire mother clutched themselves and rocked back and forth, but made no attempt to cling to the wire 'mother'. These findings confirmed the importance of contact comfort provided by the cloth mother.

Observation of the monkeys' behaviour when they were later introduced to the company of other, normally reared monkeys revealed a bleak picture. Most could not interact adequately with other monkeys; many were either aggressive or indifferent; males were unable to mate successfully; those females who did mate and produce offspring were cruel and inadequate mothers. Harlow concluded that infant monkeys cannot develop 'normal' behaviour without the presence of a live mother. However, later experiments revealed that brief exposure to other juvenile monkeys each day greatly reduced the abnormal behaviour of deprived monkeys. Could interaction with age-mates compensate for the lack of a mother?

(b)   In an attempt to assess the total importance of a mother, whether real or surrogate, Harlow and Harlow raised infant monkeys in complete isolation from both humans or other monkeys. The behaviour of these monkeys was even more bizarre than that of the surrogate-raised monkeys. They clutched their own bodies and rocked compulsively. When later exposed to other, normally-raised monkeys, they were usually apathetic and often became aggressive towards both others and themselves, biting their own arms or legs. The extent of the abnormal behaviour reflected the length of the isolation.

As a result of these experiments, Harlow claimed in 1971 that mothering is crucial for normal development in *all* primates.

(c)   More recent research has strongly questioned Harlow's earlier claims. Novak and Harlow (1975) raised infant monkeys in total isolation for a year. When the monkeys were later introduced to younger, 'therapist' monkeys, who played and interacted with them, the behaviour of the deprived monkeys became much more normal and they were able to participate effectively in all social situations.

Insights from studies of imprinting

Ethologists study the behaviour of animals in their natural habitat, from the standpoint of biology. Such naturalistic observations are considered crucial to the understanding of important behaviours such as aggression and sexual relations. Ethologists are guided by specific hypotheses in their work, and once their hypotheses have been tentatively supported from a study of the animals' natural behaviour, a specific experiment may be devised.

Konrad Lorenz, an important figure in ethology, determined that young animals such as geese and ducks follow their mothers from an early age and become permanently bonded to, or **imprinted** on her. This 'attachment' is of crucial importance to the animals' later social and mating behaviour. Lorenz showed, during the course of his experiments, that if such animals became imprinted upon a human or on some inanimate object, their later mating behaviour becomes seriously disrupted. He also proposed that such abnormal behaviour was irreversible.

In addition to studying the process and effects of imprinting, Lorenz also investigated the time during which imprinting behaviour emerged. He proposed that there was a **critical period**, or fixed time, during the first three days of life, when imprinting must occur if a lasting attachment is to result.

11

Later researchers were less convinced of the existence of such a rigid critical period in the development of imprinting. They preferred to speak instead of a **sensitive period**, a more flexible time during which imprinting is most likely to occur.

Generalising the findings of animal studies directly to humans can be a risky business. Nonetheless, the analysis offered by Harlow and the ethologists has appealed to many researchers into infant-mother relationships. One such researcher is John Bowlby (1951, 1969, 1980). His views will be considered in detail in the next section.

SELF-ASSESSMENT QUESTIONS

1   What do you understand by the term 'socialisation' as used by psychologists?

2   What is meant by 'attachment'? Give three examples of attachment behaviour in infants.

3   Briefly describe the stages in the development of attachment as proposed by Bowlby.

4   What does Schaffer mean by the 'mutual reciprocity' of the infant-mother relationship?

5   Why have the animal studies carried out by Harlow and Lorenz been of interest to researchers into the human infant-mother relationship?

6   What do you consider are the dangers of generalising the findings of animal studies to humans?

SECTION II: ATTACHMENT AND DEPRIVATION

STUDIES OF MATERNAL DEPRIVATION

In a paper to the World Health Organisation, Bowlby (1951) drew attention to the symptoms observed in institutionalised or hospitalised children. Many exhibited disturbed behaviour, were intellectually retarded, and were unable to form close relationships with others. He believed that a child deprived of the opportunity to form bonds of affection with a mother, or permanent mother substitute, during the early years of life would develop social, emotional, and/or intellectual problems in later life.

Two early studies which influenced Bowlby's views were:

1   his own account of 44 juvenile thieves in a child guidance unit, compared to 44 juveniles who were emotionally disturbed, but who

had not been accused of a crime. Bowlby observed that the former group contained many individuals who suffered from so-called 'affectionless psychopathy' (an inability to feel affection for or care about the well-being of others). Moreover, over half of the first group, compared with only two of the second, had been separated from their mothers for a period of at least a week during the first five years of life. Bowlby concluded that **maternal deprivation** was the cause of their delinquency and severe emotional disability.

2   Goldfarb's (1943) comparison of two groups of children aged between 10 and 14, 15 who had spent the first three years of life in an institution, and 15 who had spent the same period in foster homes. Compared to the 'fostered' group, the 'institutionalised' group scored lower on tests of intelligence, language and sociability. Goldfarb concluded that the inability of the institutionalised children to form an attachment with one person during the first three years of life led to their **intellectual and social retardation**.

Subsequent researchers have drawn attention to the methodological flaws in these two studies, largely arising from problems of sampling and the lack of appropriate control groups.

Maternal deprivation, according to Bowlby, could also lead to such conditions as depression, enuresis (bed-wetting) and dwarfism in children.

In his book, **Attachment and loss** (1969), Bowlby re-interpreted many of his earlier observations in the light of ethological theory. He emphasised the survival function of the human infant's need to stay close and form an attachment with its mother, and likened this attachment process to imprinting in birds. Further, he proposed that there was a 'critical period', or optimal time, probably during the first three years of life, when this primary attachment should occur.

RE-ASSESSMENTS OF MATERNAL DEPRIVATION

Bowlby's theory stimulated a great deal of research into the infant-mother relationship, some of which was referred to in the last section. Much of the evidence arising has challenged his views.

In a major re-assessment of Bowlby's work, **Rutter** (1972) supported the view that distortion of early child care may have adverse effects on psychological development. However, he objected to the term 'maternal deprivation' to cover what is probably a wide range of different problems. He urged researchers to seek more precise descriptions of 'bad' care and 'bad' effects.

Rutter distinguished between the **short-term** and **long-term** effects of 'maternal deprivation', and analysed the qualities of mothering necessary for normal development.

Short-term effects

1   Short-term effects referred to the child's immediate response to a depriving experience, and to the behaviour shown over the next few months. 'Long-term' was used to refer to effects seen some years later, either following a brief period of deprivation or after prolonged deprivation.

    Most frequently, short-term effects have been studied where a child has been admitted to hospital or a residential nursery. Most young children show an immediate reaction of excessive distress and crying (the period of '**protest**'), followed by misery and apathy (the period of '**despair**'). Finally, there is a stage where the child apparently adjusts to the situation and appears content and disinterested in its parents (the period of '**detachment**', according to Bowlby). These three phases are often referred to as the 'syndrome of distress'. The other syndrome purported to result from 'maternal deprivation' is that of developmental retardation, or slowing down of developmental growth, particularly in language and social responsiveness.

    After considering evidence on many factors which are likely to influence the child's response to deprivation (such things as age, sex, temperament, previous mother-child relationship, other separation experiences), Rutter concluded that the syndrome of distress is likely to be due to disruption of the attachment process (but not necessarily with the mother). Retardation may best be explained by the absence of appropriate, stimulating experiences.

Long-term effects

Rutter concluded that:

1   most of the long-term effects of 'maternal deprivation' are likely to be due to the lack of something (**privation**), rather than to any type of loss (**deprivation**);

2   failure to develop bonds with anyone, not just the mother, in early childhood is the main factor in the development of 'affectionless psychopathy';

3   family discord and the lack of a stable relationship with a parent are associated with later anti-social behaviour and delinquency;

4   lack of stimulation and necessary life experiences are likely to be responsible for intellectual retardation;

5   the evidence did not support Bowlby's views concerning the special importance of the bond formed with the mother. The chief bond need not be with a biological parent and it need not be with a female. He stressed the importance of a child's relationships with people other than the mother, in particular the father.

Rutter contends that the use of the term 'maternal deprivation' to explain the consequences of so many different defects in childcare is misleading. The concept should now be abandoned. Future research should aim to look at specific aspects of inadequate child care and their separate effects, and the reasons why children differ in their responses to deprivation.

Freud and Dann (1951) studied six three-year-old orphans who had spent most of their lives together in a German concentration camp. In the absence of either a mother or a father figure, the children appeared to have formed very close and warm attachments with each other. Moreover, though their behaviour was disturbed in some respects, there was no sign of 'affectionless psychopathy', the condition predicted by Bowlby to occur where children are deprived of mother-love.

Unfortunately there was no 'follow-up' study of the children's adult lives. It should also be borne in mind that this is a case study, and therefore lacks the objectivity and precision of stricter methods of study.

Schaffer and Emerson (1964) carried out a naturalistic observational study of the attachment behaviour of 60 babies. They observed that:

1   The first strong attachment to a particular person occurred around the age of seven to eight months.

2   Most children formed attachments with many people — fathers, siblings, grandparents, family friends. Schaffer and Emerson described a small group of infants whose strongest attachments were with their fathers.

3   By the age of 18 months, only 13 per cent of the babies had just one attachment figure. The remainder had formed multiple attachments.

Schaffer and Emerson concluded that 'mother' can be male or female and mothering can be shared by several people. Any person who provides a great deal of stimulation and interaction can become an attachment figure, even if they are not providing food.

Clark and Clark (1976) documented much evidence which runs counter to Bowlby's claims that infancy and early childhood years have a special, over-riding importance in social and emotional development. They propose instead that the whole of development is important, with the infancy period no more so than middle or later childhood.

Tizard and Hodges (1978), in a longitudinal study, followed the progress of a group of institutionalised children who were later adopted after the age of four. Their aim was to try to discover whether early institutional experience would affect the children's later social and emotional behaviour, even if they were adopted.

At the age of eight, it was reported by most of the adoptive parents that the children had formed strong attachments to them. However, many parents reported that the children had some emotional problems: they were often difficult to manage and at school were quarrelsome and unpopular with their peers.

Tizard concluded that:

1   the first two years of life appeared to be critical in shaping some aspects of later development; the early institutional experiences of the children did appear to have caused some behavioural problems;

2   the possibility should be borne in mind that some of the children might be genetically disposed to emotional instability, or had mothers who were under stress during pregnancy;

3   most children had formed attachments with adoptive parents and there was little to support Bowlby's claims of an early 'critical period' for the formation of attachments.

ENRICHMENT

Tizard's study, and others like it, provide an answer to the question of whether environmental improvement (or enrichment) which does not occur until middle or later childhood can be beneficial to a child's social and emotional development. The evidence suggests that it can. This has been borne out by studies of children from severely disturbed homes who later became part of a stable and harmonious family. In addition, a number of studies demonstrate that the quality of the environment during adolescence, or even adult life, may still influence people's behaviour and social relationships.

CROSS-CULTURAL STUDIES OF ATTACHMENT

Ainsworth (1967) spent several months observing patterns of attachment in infants of the Ganda tribe in Uganda. Her study provided striking support for Bowlby's description of the course of attachment behaviour. Most of the babies were clearly attached to their mothers by around six months; most began to fear strangers during the last three months of their first year. However, the babies were cared for by several adults in addition to their mothers, and most formed attachments simultaneously with several people.

In many **Israeli kibbutzim**, children live separately from their parents and are cared for in a children's house from early infancy by a metapalet, or children's nurse. Research suggests that such children nevertheless appear to form stronger attachments to their mothers than to the caretakers with whom they spend so much time (Fox 1977). The babies also develop strong bonds with their own infant peers which leads to a much greater social involvement than is usually observed in such young children.

THE ROLE OF THE FATHER

Most of the studies described earlier have focused upon the mother/child relationship, and in each case the mothering has been carried out by a female. But what of fathers? Over the last decade or so much research has examined infant/father attachments.

An early study carried out in a maternity ward showed that there was little difference between the reactions of mothers and fathers towards their babies. Kotelchuk demonstrated that infants were equally upset in the presence of a stranger whether mother or father left the room. Lamb detected few differences in signs of attachment when children played alone, first with one parent and then the other. However, when both parents are present, most children are likely to display stronger attachment to the mother. Studies by Lamb drew attention to differences in the ways in which mothers and fathers interact with children. Typically, fathers play more vigorously with their children than mothers do; they do not sit as close and they talk to them in more adult language. Mothers tend to interact with their infants in a gentler, more low-key fashion. Belsky (1979) contends that mothers and fathers play different but complementary roles in the lives of children.

CONCLUSIONS

Much of the research reviewed in this chapter has challenged Bowlby's account of attachment and deprivation. While the evidence overwhelmingly supports the importance of deprivation and disadvantage as adverse influences on children's psychological development, it appears that humans are far more flexible than Bowlby suggests. A single, female, mothering-figure is not essential to healthy development; research has confirmed the importance of a child's relationships with people other than the mother.

Bowlby's likening of the human infant-mother relationship to animal imprinting seems strained. There is little firm evidence to support a 'critical period' for the formation of attachment. While the first few years of life do appear to be important for bond formation and social development, the evidence suggests that experiences at all ages can have an impact.

Signposts: In an updating of his earlier work, Rutter highlights those issues which have been more recently investigated and which are likely to continue to be the focus of research. Among these are:

1   the reciprocal nature of parent/child interactions (see Schaffer (1977) in Section I) and the processes through which such relationships develop;

" PERSONALLY, I THINK THAT
NURSERY SCHOOL PUTS **TOO** MUCH
EMPHASIS ON CREATIVE PLAY
WITH TOY MONEY ! "

2   links between childhood experiences and parents' behaviour;

3   the effects of factors outside the home, including the importance of school experiences;

4   individual differences in children's responses to stress and deprivation, i.e. the reasons why some children develop normally despite adverse experiences.

SELF-ASSESSMENT QUESTIONS

1   Outline Bowlby's view on the probable effects of maternal deprivation in children.

2   How, according to Bowlby, does a knowledge of imprinting in animals inform our understanding of attachment in human infants?

3   Distinguish between the short-term and the long-term effects of 'maternal deprivation' in children. Explain Rutter's use of the terms 'privation' and 'deprivation'.

4   Outline two studies which have challenged Bowlby's views.

5   What conclusions would you draw about attachment in human infants in the light of the research reviewed?

6   What comparisons might be made between the behaviour of the late-adopted children in Tizard's study, and that of the rehabilitated monkeys in the study by Harlow and Novak?

SECTION III: PLAY

WHAT IS PLAY?

Play is a characteristic part of the behaviour of all normal, healthy children. It appears to have important implications for a child's psychological development. This section aims to consider the nature and functions of play, and its role in development.

Gardner (1982) believes the purposes of play in the development of the child to be:

> . . . greater mastery of the world, more adequate coping with problems and fears, superior understanding of oneself and one's relationship to the world, an initial exploration of the relations between reality and fantasy, an arena in which intuitive, semi-logical forms of thought can be freely tested.

From the child's point of view, the purpose of play is pure pleasure — enjoyment 'for its own sake', with no conscious practical or biological goals involved.

Socially, there is a clear developmental sequence in a child's style of play in the early years.

1   Until the age of 18 months to two years, there is much **solitary play** with objects such as toys.

2   The three year old is more likely to indulge in **parallel play**, playing alongside other children, sometimes watching and imitating, but not truly interacting.

3   Around the age of four, play becomes increasingly **social** and simple interactions take place. Initially these interactions are quite rigid, but soon involve 'give and take' in the form of turn-taking and co-operation.

Psychologists have categorised many different activities as 'play'. There is the physical, repetitive play of the one year old, the fantasy and make-believe of the three year old, the more purposeful and structured play of the older child. Painting, playing with bricks, experimenting with sand and water, kicking a football, exploring a new object — all are subsumed under the heading of 'play'.

The range and diversity of all these activities have presented psychologists with a dilemma in seeking to describe and explain behaviour associated with play, particularly during early childhood. Some disagreement exists about the activities which should be categorised as play.

SOME THEORIES OF PLAY

Piaget firmly links the development of play with the development of thought (see Chapter 3) and contends that a child's developmental level may be inferred in part from its play. He proposes three broad stages of play activity.

1   **Mastery play** corresponds to the sensory-motor stage of development (birth to two approximately). The emphasis is on practice and control of movements, and on exploration of objects through sight and touch. The child's play activity contains many repetitive movements which are indulged in for the simple pleasure of demonstrating her/his own developing mastery of the skills involved.

2   **Symbolic play** coincides with the pre-operational stage (approximately two to seven). The child employs fantasy and make-believe in play and delights in using one object to symbolise another

— so a chair may become a motor car, a sheet a fashionable dress.

3   **Play with rules** characterises the operational stages (from about seven onwards). The child's developing thought processes become more logical and play involves the use of rules and procedures.

Piaget proposes that play is an expression of the process of **assimilation**, where the child is attempting to take knowledge of the world around and change it to fit in with her/his own understanding and experience.

    Bruner (1976) stresses the learning potential of play. He views play as a means of attaining physical and cognitive skills in young children. Play involves experimentation with smaller actions which may later be combined into a more complex, higher order skill. Thus the two-year old, given a set of construction toys, will initially explore and handle individual pieces. Over a period of time, the child will experiment with possible uses and combinations until eventually she/he will be able to assemble complete constructions with confidence. This kind of play allows the child to understand such things as spatial relations and mechanics in a relaxed, non-threatening setting. Thus play contributes to problem-solving and an understanding of the use of tools.

    Vygotsky (1967) sees play as a leading contributor to over-all development. Vygotsky emphasises particularly the rules of play. Confronted with a problem, the child unconsciously devises a make-believe situation which is easier to cope with. Such a 'game' involves the use of set rules and procedures which enable the child to take an object from its familiar context and believe that it is something else — so a broom handle can become a horse and the 'rules' of the game allow the child to behave in a manner which is removed from everyday reality.

    Vygotsky believes that play creates a 'zone of potential development' in which the child can operate at a level which is above that for its normal age; for instance, performing some of the movements of writing for the first time. One way of assessing a child's potential development at a particular time is to note the distance between the levels of activity reached during play and those of its customary behaviour.

    Freud's psychodynamic theory of development views play as a means of relieving pent-up emotions. Children may use play to explore and cope with their feelings about life, and work out their fears and anxieties (catharsis) in a safe situation. Play can thus be seen both as a defence against problems and as a coping behaviour.

    Erikson (1963), a neo-Freudian, contends that:

> the child's play is the infantile form of the human ability to deal with experience by creating model situations and to master reality by experiment and planning.

The psychodynamic approach to play is characterised in the use of **play therapy** to treat disturbed children. The basic assumption is that the child's play is a reflection of her/his unconscious mind. During therapy the child is allowed to play in a safe, undemanding situation with objects such as dolls, buildings, etc. Through play sessions the child can act out and come to terms with anxieties.

STUDIES OF PLAY

Hutt (1966) carried out a study in which she investigated **exploratory play**. Exploration is explained as an activity during which a child may investigate objects and events in the environment and/or features of her/his own physical abilities. It has been questioned whether exploratory behaviour should be identified as play.

Hutt studied exploratory behaviour in a formal experiment. Children aged three to five were presented with a novel and complex object in the form of a red, metal box with four brass legs and topped with a lever which, when moved, activated various novel auditory or visual stimuli. Also present were five familiar toys. Typically, at first, a child concentrated on trying to find out what the novel object could do. This sequence was followed by an attempt to use the object as part of a game, while at the same time making use of the familiar toys. Once the child had become familiar with the object, she/he would investigate it further only if a new feature, for example a new sight or sound, was discovered.

Hutt distinguished between the earlier, exploratory behaviour and the later play behaviour. She proposes that **specific exploration** should be differentiated from **diverse exploration**, and that only the latter might be categorised as play.

In a follow-up to this study, Hutt and Bhavnani revisited the children whose exploratory behaviour had been studied. They found that non-exploring in early childhood relates to lack of curiosity and adventure in boys, and to problems of personality and social adjustment for girls. Those children who had been earlier categorised as active explorers were more likely to be judged as independent and curious by their teachers and more likely to score high on tests of creativity. Hutt proposes a relation between one form of exploration (as investigated in this study) and subsequent personality and cognitive style.

Sylva *et al.* (1980) carried out a naturalistic observational study of the play of pre-school children in Oxfordshire play groups and nursery schools. They were particularly concerned to investigate how play may contribute to cognitive development. **Elaborated play** was distinguished as rich play which challenges the child and stimulates more complex activity which involves the child's fullest capacities. Elaborated play has two important characteristics.

1   It has a clear goal and some means for its achievement.

2   It has 'real world feedback', i.e. the child is able to assess her/his own progress without referring to anyone else.

FINDINGS

1   The richest, most elaborated and extended play occurs in building and construction activities, drawing and art and doing puzzles. These activities also encourage the child to concentrate for longer periods.

2   Somewhat behind these activities is play involving pretending, small-scale toys, sand and dough.

3   Less elaborated play, such as informal, impromptu games and 'horsing around', appears to serve the functions of release of tension and social contact.

4   Young children play longer and better when they operate in pairs rather than alone or in larger groups. The presence of an adult nearby for assurance or brief comment, but not managing, improves the quality of play.

The findings of Sylva's study have important implications for the organisation and staffing of nursery schools and playgroups.

FOOTNOTE

This section has offered a brief selection of theories and studies of children's play and its significance in development. Further detailed and systematic research must be carried out before a full understanding can be reached of the diverse and varied activities at present categorised as play.

SELF-ASSESSMENT QUESTIONS

1   What do you understand by 'play'?

2   What is 'exploratory play'?

3   Discuss briefly one study of play.

4   List some of the differences you might observe between the play of three-year-old children and the play of eight-year-old children.

5   Discuss theory and evidence which suggest that play contributes to cognitive development. What kinds of play may be most effective?

6   What is the major problem which faces psychologists who seek to describe and explain the functions of play?

FURTHER READING

Bowlby J **Attachment & loss: I — Attachment**. Hogarth Press 1969.

Bruner J S **Under five in Britain**. Grant McIntyre 1980.

Clarke A M & A D Clarke **Early experience: myth & evidence**. Open Books 1976.

Garvey C **Play**. Fontana/Open Books 1977.

Rutter M **Maternal deprivation re-assessed**. Penguin Books 1981.

Schaffer H R **Mothering**. Fontana/Open Books London 1977.

Stern D N **The first relationship: infant and mother**. Fontana/Open Books London 1977.

Chapter 3

Cognitive Development

At the end of this chapter, you should be able to:

1   describe Piaget's theory of cognitive development;

2   evaluate Piaget's theory in the light of subsequent research;

3   consider the educational implications of Piaget's theory;

4   describe Bruner's theory of cognitive development and consider some educational implications;

5   show an appreciation of the information-processing approach to cognitive development;

6   critically evaluate theories of language acquisition.

INTRODUCTION

The term cognitive, which derives from the Latin *cognosco* (to know), refers to all those psychological activities involved in the acquisition, processing, organisation and use of knowledge — in other words, all those abilities associated with thinking and knowing. The cognitive processes of perception and memory have been the most widely studied . Cognitive abilities include also a child's measured intelligence, her/his levels of thinking and even, to some extent, her/his creativity and the way in which she/he conducts interpersonal relationships. Since language is the medium through which thinking usually takes place, and since much intelligent and creative activity is expressed through language, this too is usually regarded as a cognitive activity.

Two key questions dominate the study of cognitive development.

1   What changes in cognitive functioning occur as the child grows older?

2   What factors may be responsible for these changes?

The best known and most influential approach to these questions is that of the Swiss biologist-turned-psychologist, Jean Piaget. Piaget's theory focuses mainly on logical thinking, reasoning and problem-solving, and is less directly concerned with processes such as perception and memory.

ISSUES IN THE STUDY OF CHILD DEVELOPMENT

Before considering theories of cognitive development it is important to note two major issues, or controversies, which relate to the study of child development, and which are particularly pertinent when considering the study of cognitive development.

1 Maturation v learning

The first issue arises from the fact that we are still unable to unravel the interaction between maturation — the biological changes that take place within the individual throughout his life — and learning — the changes that come about through the experiences the individual has with the world about him/her. Although most psychologists believe that social interactions between the child and the people around her/him, and stimulation from objects and events in his/her environment contribute substantially to cognitive development, it may be that some intellectual progress stems largely from the development of the central nervous system. Physically handicapped children who are unable to play with toys or move freely about their environment show normal development of many cognitive abilities. There is, however, also evidence that the quality of the environment experienced by children can be a factor which affects the speed with which their intellect develops. Children in remote and deprived areas of the world, who live in an unstimulating environment without toys, may be substantially behind western children in developing some intellectual capacities (Kagan *et al.* 1979).

2 Competence and performance

The second important issue has concerned many researchers whose work has involved the study of young children. A problem sometimes arises in distinguishing between what children actually know and can do — that is, their competence — and the extent to which children make use of their ability to deal with tasks and problems — that is, their performance. Children may possess abilities that they do not use in some situations.

The problem of competence and performance can be illustrated in a study in which pre-school children were asked to sort objects belonging to different categories (vehicles, trees, people, furniture). They were asked to put objects belonging to the same category either into separate plastic bags or onto different pieces of paper. The childen were found to be more successful in sorting objects when asked to place them in bags than when asked to place them on pieces of paper. Hence, a child who failed to put the objects representing trees onto one piece of paper — a failure in performance — probably possessed the competence of understanding the concept we call trees, but did not demonstrate it (Markman *et al.* 1981).

The reasons why a child's performance may not adequately reflect his/her competence are complex and are only just starting to be understood by investigators. The context and relevance of the situation in which the child is operating, his/her interpretation of the language used by the experimenter, and his/her assumptions about the intentions of the experimenter are all factors which may affect the child's performance. (See the discussion of the work of Bryant and Donaldson later in this chapter.)

SECTION I:
PIAGET'S THEORY OF COGNITIVE DEVELOPMENT

Most psychologists would agree that Jean Piaget was the most influential developmental psychologist of the 20th century. Largely as a result of his work, cognition has been a major focus in child development research since the late 1950s when his work was translated from French into English.

For over half a century Piaget made detailed observations of children's activities, talked to children, listened to them talking to each other, and devised and presented many 'tests' of children's thinking. His methods of study, which included the **clinical interview** and **naturalistic observation** (see Chapter 1), were in sharp contrast to the rigorous and strictly controlled methods used by the Behaviourists. In his studies, Piaget did not manipulate variables in the manner of formal experiments. His early research programme attempted instead to describe the kinds of thinking characteristic of children up to adolescence. Further, Piaget's interest was not in the uniqueness of individual children, but rather in the similarities between children of roughly equivalent ages.

Piaget's findings led him to propose a theory of how children form the concepts involved in thinking — that is, a theory which suggests that children develop more sophisticated ways of thinking mainly as a consequence of maturation.

A concept is the idea an individual has about a particular class of objects (including animate objects) or events, grouped together on the basis of the things they have in common. It is through concepts that we are able to think about and make sense of the world. Thus a small child will have a concept of 'daddy', 'dog' or 'table', of 'softness' and 'hardness' of 'small things' and 'large things' of 'more than' and 'less than'. When children encounter new objects and experiences, they try to make sense of them by fitting them into their existing concepts. Consider the two-year old girl who has formed the concept of 'bird' as an object that flies in the sky. One day she sees her first aeroplane and tries to link it to her concept of 'bird'. But the noise, the size and the shape do not fit her existing concept. If she questions her parents, they will provide a new word and explain the differences between birds and aeroplanes, therefore allowing the child to create a new concept.

Piaget believed that the way in which we are able to form and deal with concepts changes as we move through childhood into adolescence. A child's thinking is not simply a less well informed version of an adult's, but differs from it in a number of important ways which are discussed below.

SCHEMATA AND OPERATIONS
(VARIANT COGNITIVE STRUCTURES)

Piaget saw the structure of the intellect in terms of **schemata** and **operations**. A schema is the internal representation of some specific physical or mental action. The new born child, he believes, is endowed with a number of innate schemata which correspond to reflex responses, for example the looking schema, the grasping schema, the sucking schema and so on. As the child develops, these innate schemata integrate with each other and become more elaborate, and entirely new schemata are formed as the child responds to his/her environment.

Fundamental to intelligence are schemata consisting of knowledge about things/events and knowledge of how to do things. In any intellectual or physical act, there is always a schema of some kind present, a kind of cognitive plan which the individual uses to deal with a particular problem.

An operation is a higher order mental structure which is not present at birth, and is usually not acquired until middle childhood. An operation involves the child in knowing more complex rules about how the environment works. It has the characteristic of being **reversible**. This means that an operation can be regarded as a mental activity which can be reversed — done backwards, so to speak. The rules of arithmetic involve operations which are reversible. For example, a child of five will readily understand the process of addition $(2+3=5)$ but will not appreciate that this process is reversible by subtraction $(5-3=2)$. The older child who is capable of operational thinking will recognise that addition is reversible by subtraction and division is reversible by multiplication.

Consider another example of operational thinking. Read experiment 1 on page 32. When asked the final question, 'Does the 'sausage' have the same amount of plasticine as the 'cake'?', the answer given by a child of five is usually very different from the answer given by a child of seven or eight. The older child will reply without hesitation 'of course they are the same'. The younger child typically says that the 'sausage' now contains more plasticine than the 'cake'. The younger child's thinking seems to be dominated by the appearance of objects. Moreover, she/he is not capable of performing the mental operation of reversibility, or mentally reversing the moulding of the 'sausage'.

Children's cognitive structures change as they grow older. Hence, Piaget terms 'schemata' and 'operations' **variant cognitive structures**.

ADAPTATION TO THE ENVIRONMENT
(INVARIANT FUNCTIONS)

Piaget based his theory firmly within a biological framework, and

adaptation is a key concept. In order to survive, every individual must adapt to the demands of the environment.

Intellectual development is seen as the adaptation of cognitive structures (schemata and operations) to meet the demands of the environment. Such adaptation takes place through the processes of **assimilation** and **accommodation**. Assimilation refers to the process whereby a new object or idea is understood in terms of concepts or actions (schemata) the child already possesses. Accommodation is a complementary process which enables all individuals to modify concepts and actions to fit new situations, objects or information.

Consider again the example described above of the child who first encounters an aeroplane. Her initial interpretation of it as a bird is an example of assimilation — she assimilates the aeroplane into her schema of 'bird'. On acquiring new information about the characteristics of an aeroplane, she accommodates to the new situation and consequently develops a new schema.

The twin processes of assimilation and accommodation continue throughout life as we adapt our behaviour and ideas to changing circumstances. Assimilation is the process that enables an individual to deal with new situations and new problems by using existing schemata. Accommodation, on the other hand, is the process which involves the changing of existing schemata or the development of new schemata. It is because of the unchanging nature of these processes that Piaget referred to assimilation and accommodation as **invariant functions**.

Before a child has acquired new knowledge, he/she is in a state of what Piaget called **equilibrium** (or cognitive harmony). When this state of equilibrium is disturbed — that is when something new or demanding is encountered — the processes of assimilation and accommodation function to restore it. Piaget proposes a process of **equilibration** which acts to ensure that accommodation is consolidated via assimilation, and that a balance is maintained between the two. In this way, mental structures change and cognitive ability gradually progresses.

PIAGET'S DEVELOPMENTAL STAGES

Piaget has identified a number of distinct stages of intellectual development. He proposes that the child moves through each of these stages in turn, in the sequence and at approximately the ages shown below. The speed at which he/she moves through each stage, although influenced by the child's particular experiences, is essentially controlled by biologically determined maturational processes. The process cannot be hastened — a child must be maturationally ready before she or he can move from one stage to the next. At each stage new, more sophisticated levels of thinking are added to the child's cognitive repertoire.

Stage 1 Sensori-Motor (approximately birth to two years)

In this stage the child experiences his/her world mainly through his/her **immediate perceptions** and through **physical activity**, without thought as adults know it. For example, not until about eight months does a child have any concept of the **permanence of objects**. Until then, out of sight is out of mind, and the child will not attempt to look for a previously visible object which is placed out of sight as she/he watches. The child's thinking is dominated by the 'here and now'. With the acquisition of the object concept and when other means of knowing, such as memory and language, are available to him or her, the sensori-motor stage is at an end. The child can now anticipate the future and think about the past.

Stage 2 Pre-operational (approximately two to seven years)

This is the stage that has been most extensively studied by Piaget. It marks a long period of transition which culminates in the emergence of operational thinking. With the development of language the child is now capable of symbolic thought, though, Piaget argues, the child's intellectual capabilities are still largely dominated by his/her perceptions, rather than by a conceptual grasp of situations and events.

Piaget describes a number of limitations to a child's thinking which exist at this stage of development. These limitations are described below.

1 **Egocentrism** refers to the child's inability to see the world from anything but his/her own point of view. The child is not capable of understanding that there can be viewpoints other than his/her own. Thus, if a small boy is asked to say what someone sitting on the other side of a room is able to see, he will describe things from his own perspective only; a little girl may tell you that she has a sister, but will strenuously deny that her sister has a sister!

   Figure 1 illustrates Piaget's famous 'three mountains task' which was designed to illustrate the egocentrism of young children.

2 **Centration** involves attending to (centring on) only one feature of a situation and ignoring others, no matter how relevant. The child's inability to de-centre is apparent in Piaget's famous **conservation** experiments, some of which are described in Figure 2.

   In experiment 1 the younger pre-operational child will exhibit an inability to conserve — that is, will be unable to grasp the fact that the amount of plasticine remains the same even though the appearance of one may change. Similarly, in experiment 2, even though the child has agreed that the two 'fat' beakers contain the same amount of liquid, when the contents of one are poured into a tall, thin beaker, the child will now usually contend that we have more liquid than before, simply because the level has risen higher. This illustrates an inability to conserve volume. In experiment 3, the

Figure 1

Piaget's 'mountains task' showing three mountains viewed (a) from the front and (b) from the top

(a)

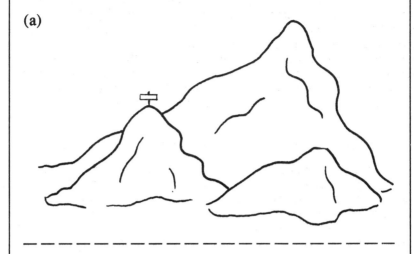

(b)

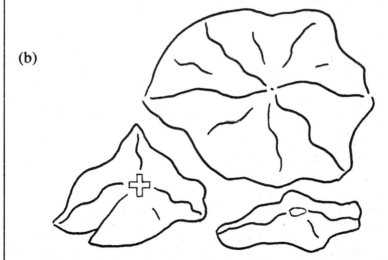

The child is asked to select from a series of photographs of the model landscape one that corresponds to a view different to his own. A child under eight does not seem to be able to imagine what other views would be like.

Figure 2

Experiment 1   **Conservation of substance**

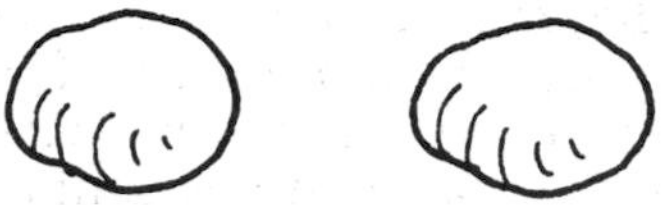

1. The child is shown two identical balls of plasticine and is asked "Are these two 'cakes' the same?".

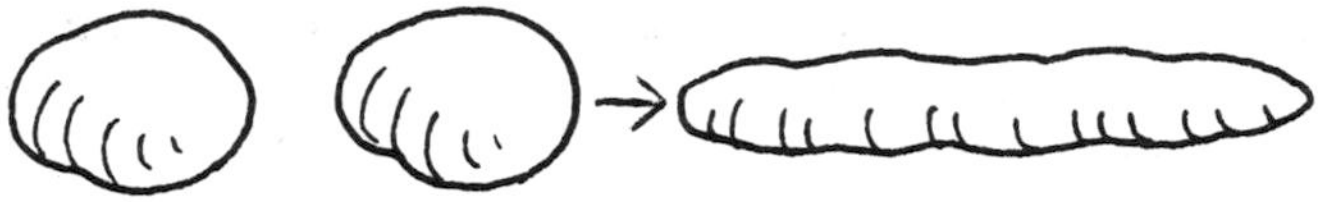

2. The experimenter rolls out one ball of plasticine into a 'sausage' shape. The child is asked "Does the sausage have the same amount of plasticine as the 'cake'?".

Experiment 2   **Conservation of volume**

(a)   (b)

1. The child is shown a short, 'fat' beaker (a) containing milk and is asked to pour milk from a jug into a second identical beaker (b) until it has the same amount of milk as the first beaker. The child agrees that the amount of milk in each beaker is identical.

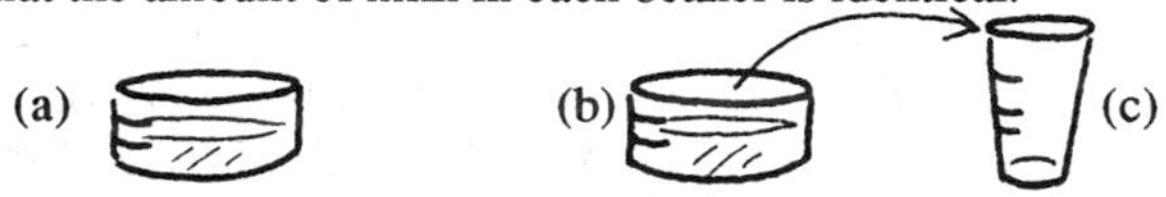

(a)   (b)   (c)

2. The child is then shown a tall 'thin' beaker and is asked to pour the contents of one of the original beakers into it. He is then asked "Is there the same in (c) as there is in (a)?".

Experiment 3   **Conservation of number**

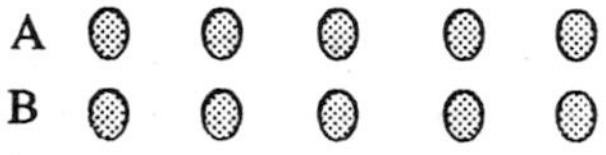

A   ⊛   ⊛   ⊛   ⊛   ⊛
B   ⊛   ⊛   ⊛   ⊛   ⊛

1. The child is shown counters placed in two identical rows (A and B) The child agrees that the two rows have the same number of counters.

A   ⊛   ⊛   ⊛   ⊛   ⊛
B   ⊛⊛⊛⊛⊛

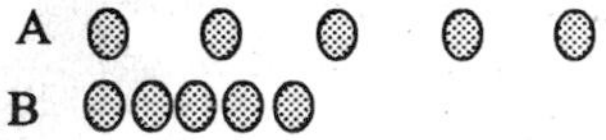

2. The experimenter 'bunches up' the counters in row B. The child is asked "Do the two rows still contain the same number of counters?".

pre-operational child will claim that the two rows in part 2 of the experiment do not now contain the same number of counters.

All these conservation experiments are the same in that they first involve a phase in which the child is presented with two entities and is asked to agree that they are 'the same'. Then the appearance of one entity is transformed while the child watches. The child is then asked to judge whether the two things are still the same. Piaget carried out similar experiments with area, length, weight and so on.

3   **Irreversibility** - the conservation experiments also show the inability of the pre-operational child to work backwards mentally to her/his starting point. Look back to page 28 and re-read the discussion of the importance of reversibility to the development of operational thinking.

Stage 3 Concrete operations (approximately 7-11 years)

The main features of this stage are

1   the acquisition of reversible thinking, and

2   the ability to de-centre.

Hence, the child confronted with conservation tasks is capable of understanding the concept of invariance, partly because she or he realises that the transformation of shape, volume, spatial distributions, etc. are capable of being reversed, and partly because his/her thinking is no longer dominated by only one feature of a situation. Piaget maintains that conservation takes place in a definite order, with the conservation of number coming first at approximately 6-7 years and conservation of volume being achieved last at about 11 or 12 years of age. The child also becomes less egocentric, and is now capable of seeing objects and events from the viewpoint of another.

Another important feature of this stage is the child's increasing ability to handle such concepts as **classification** - the ability to group objects together logically in terms of their common characteristics — and **seriation** - the ability to arrange items in rank order in terms, for example, of their colour or size.

The stage of concrete operations is so-called because the child needs to manipulate and experiment with real objects, in order to solve problems in a logical way. For example, the child at this stage will have difficulty dealing with the verbal problem 'Joan is taller than Susan; Joan is smaller than Mary; who is the smallest?' in his head, but would have no difficulty if given three dolls to represent Joan, Susan and Mary.

Stage 4 Formal Operations (approximately 11 years onwards)

This stage marks the emergence of the ability to reason in the abstract without having to rely on concrete objects or events. The child's thinking increasingly resembles that of the adult. She/he is able to solve a problem in his head by systematically testing out several propositions, by isolating such propositions and at the same time considering their inter-relatedness.

Figure 3 illustrates Piaget's 'pendulum task', which was used to investigate formal operational thinking.

Figure 3

Piaget's 'pendulum task' designed to investigate formal operational thinking

The child is given a length of string suspended from a hook and several weights. He is told he can vary the length of the string, change the weight and vary the strength of 'push'. His task is to find out which of these different factors affects the time taken to complete one swing of the pendulum.

The pre-operational child typically thinks the strength of 'push' is the only important factor.

The concrete operational child will attempt to investigate the different factors - different weights, shorter or longer string, etc., but does so randomly rather than systematically.

The formal operational child systematically tests each factor. He sets up a hypothesis that one or the other factor is important and tests it out until all possibilities have been investigated.

EVALUATING PIAGET'S THEORY AND RESEARCH

Child psychology has been greatly influenced by Piaget.

> During the long period when his work was largely ignored by most psychologists, the subject tended to treat children either as members of various remote and incomprehensible tribes, or as slightly superior rats (Bryant 1982).

It was because of Piaget's work that the traditional view of the child as a passive being, moulded by the experiences of his/her environment, was replaced by the view of the child as a curious and active seeker of

34

knowledge and stimulation . Moreover, Piaget's theories have made a major impact in the field of education and have greatly influenced the way children are taught, particularly at the primary school level.

Many of the main tenets of Piaget's theory are accepted by most psychologists — for example the interactionist view that cognitive development depends on both maturation and experience of the environment. Nonetheless, the theory has not been without its critics. Many experts have pointed out weaknesses in the theory and have questioned some of Piaget's interpretations of children's behaviour. However, a great deal of the research arising from such criticisms has been extremely productive '. . . much of our most exciting information about intellectual development comes from experimenters whose starting-point was either a doubt about one or other of Piaget's conclusions, or a desire to defend him against his critics' (Bryant 1982). Some of the controversies surrounding Piaget's work include the following.

1 Methodological Considerations

(a) Piaget's reliance on the clinical interview method has been criticised. It has been suggested that because there were no set questions and no standard method of presentation, there may have been a tendency to 'lead' children into views that were not strictly their own. Piaget himself was aware of these problems and much of his later work employed more strictly controlled methods.

(b) Bryant (1974) argued that the design of many Piagetian tasks made it very difficult for children to give correct answers. Piaget, he felt, may have overestimated the language and memory skills of young children. By a slight rewording of a Piagetian question or the use of a more 'realistic' example, Bryant showed that children under five were capable of more sophisticated thought than Piaget claimed.

2 Object Permanence

In a series of experiments with babies, Bower showed that some infants as young as four to six weeks have some ability to appreciate the existence of objects which disappear from view.

3 Egocentricity

Piaget's 'mountains task' was designed to assess whether a child can take the point of view of another person. Using this model, Piaget claimed that children under about eight years do not perform successfully. Margaret Donaldson (1978) describes a series of experiments, carried out by her colleagues, which shows that young children between three and a half and five years old are quite capable of appreciating the view point of another person. Figure 4 contains a description of the 'naughty boy hiding from the policeman' task carried out by Hughes (1975).

Figure 4

A model shown to pre-school children in an experiment designed to investigate egocentricity (Donaldson 1978)

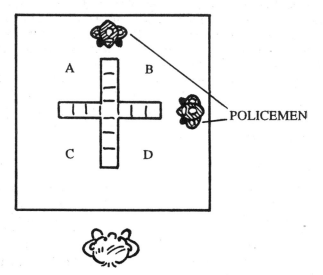

CHILD

1. Two 'walls' are set up to form a cross.

2. A 'policeman' doll is placed on the model so that he can see the areas marked A and C, but cannot see B and D because they are obstructed by the wall.

3. The child is given a 'boy' doll and asked to place it on the model where the policeman cannot see it.

4. The task is repeated several times using two police man dolls which are placed in varying positions on the model. On each occasion the child is asked to place the boy where the policemen cannot see him.

5. Ninety per cent of the children tested placed the 'boy' doll correctly so that neither 'policeman' could see it.

From **Children's minds** Donaldson (1978), Norton.

Why should the experiment described by Donaldson produce findings which were so different to those of Piaget when he used the 'mountains task'? Firstly, in Donaldson's experiment, a great deal of care was taken to ensure that the children fully understood the task, and in particular, the meaning of 'to hide'. Secondly, Donaldson claimed that the 'policeman' task 'made sense' to the child and that its realism and interest-value captured the child's imagination. '. . . the task requires the child to act in ways which are in line with certain very basic human purposes (escape and pursuit). It makes human sense . . . in this context, he shows none of the difficulty in 'decentring' which Piaget ascribes to him . . . the 'mountains task' is abstract in a psychologically very important sense, in the sense that it is abstracted from all basic human purposes and feelings and endeavours'. (Donaldson 1978)

4   **Conservation**

Many psychologists have contested Piaget's claim that children in the pre-operational stage are unable to conserve. It has been pointed out that it is by no means certain that young children use and interpret words in the same way as adults do and failure in conservation tasks may, in some cases, be accounted for in terms of the difficulties children experience with word meanings, for example 'less than' and 'more than' and so on.

As in the 'policeman' task, context too may be an important factor in conservation experiments. In a replication of one of Piaget's number tasks, McGarrigle (reported in Donaldson 1978) found, as did Piaget, that few children under six appeared to understand conservation of number (refer back to Experiment 3 in Figure 2). However, the experiment was repeated, but this time a 'naughty' teddy bear was introduced, who proceeded to re-arrange one row of counters while 'messing about'. When asked on this occasion if both rows contained the same number, a large proportion (63 per cent) of the children gave the correct answer, indicating their ability to conserve number.

Why should 'naughty teddy' have made such a difference? Donaldson argues that in the earlier experiment, the child may have thought that because the experimenter (an important adult) had re-arranged the counters, it seemed reasonable to assume that something must have changed. This experiment and the policeman task are illustrations of the problematical nature of the relationship between a child's competence and his performance, discussed earlier.

5   **The concept of stages**

Piaget proposed that the development of the intellect occurs in 'clear cut'; qualitatively different stages, each of which builds upon and replaces the level of adaptation reached in a previous stage. Some later investigators claim that their findings support this view of stage-like changes in cognitive behaviour (Neimark 1975). Other investigators are more critical and argue that discontinuous, step-like changes in cognitive development are unlikely (Keating 1980) and that development proceeds in a continuous manner.

Despite all these criticisms of Piaget's work, it is noteworthy that the vast majority of critical studies contain a tribute to the man whose great intellectual scope provided such a monumental contribution to our understanding of child development. The task now being undertaken by contemporary psychologists is that of extending and modifying his work.

IMPLICATIONS OF PIAGET'S THEORY FOR EDUCATION

Although Piaget's theory was not directly concerned with what goes on in the classroom, his work has had a major impact on the way children are taught, particularly at the primary school level. Some of the educational implications of his theory are outlined below.

1   Because of Piaget, parents and teachers are aware that a child's intellect is qualitatively different to that of an adult. Teachers should be sensitive to the child's level of development and her/his ability to understand and deal with concepts of varying kinds. Asking a child to cope with tasks or solve problems before she/he is **ready** to deal with the concepts involved will result in confusion and distress and may prevent the child from ever fully appreciating some concepts.

2   Piaget emphasises the importance of active participation and interaction with the environment. The teacher should provide an appropriate environment in the form of rich and varied materials and activities which will stimulate the child's natural curiosity. Opportunities to **learn by discovery** will encourage children to explore the environment and learn through their own activities.

3   Children below the formal operational level must be introduced to new concepts through **concrete objects**, building up gradually, where appropriate, to more abstract reasoning.

4   In order for a child to accommodate new ideas and experiences, the teacher must allow her/him first to assimilate them. New concepts should therefore be linked to what the child knows and has experienced already.

SELF-ASSESSMENT QUESTIONS

1   Discuss two controversial issues which relate to the study of cognitive development.

2   Briefly describe Piaget's methods of investigating children's thought processes.

3   Define the terms 'schema' and 'operation' as used by Piaget. Why are these known as 'variant cognitive structures'?

4   Briefly explain the processes of assimilation and accommodation.

5   List the key features of children's thought processes at each of Piaget's developmental stages. What factor did Piaget believe principally governs the speed at which children progress through these stages?

6   Evaluate Piaget's theory in the light of more recent research.

7   Discuss some of the educational implications of Piaget's theory.

SECTION II:
BRUNER'S THEORY OF COGNITIVE DEVELOPMENT

The American psychologist, Jerome Bruner (1964), has made a significant contribution to our knowledge of cognitive development. He suggests that children develop three main ways of internally representing the environment to themselves on their way to acquiring the mature thought processes of the adult. These three **modes of representation** are the **enactive**, the **iconic** and the **symbolic**.

In the **enactive mode**, thinking is based entirely on physical actions and uses neither imagery nor words. For a baby playing with a toy, the movement involved becomes her/his internal representation of the toy. Enactive representation operates throughout life and is apparent in many physical activities, for example, throwing a ball, swimming, cycling, which we learn by doing and which we do not represent internally through language or images.

When a child becomes capable of representing the environment through mental images, **iconic representation** is possible. These mental images may be visual, auditory, olfactory or tactile. They provide a means whereby children may experience and build up a picture of the environment, even though they may be unable to describe it in words.

Finally, the transition from the iconic to the **symbolic mode** occurs and the child is able to represent the environment through language and later through other symbolic systems such as number and music. Symbolic representation leads to thought of a much more flexible and abstract kind, allowing the individual not only to represent reality but to manipulate and transform it.

A classic experiment by Bruner and Kenny exemplifies the limitations of iconic thinking. Children from five to seven were shown an arrangement of glass tumblers which were placed on a board in order

Figure 5

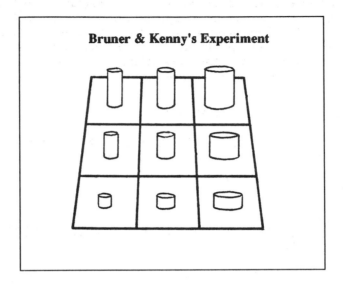

Bruner & Kenny's Experiment

according to height and diameter. (See figure 5) When the glasses were removed, all the children were capable of replacing them in the correct positions. Then the glasses were removed and one glass was replaced on the board, but in a different position. The children were asked to replace the rest of the glasses so as to retain the original pattern. The older children, who were capable of symbolic thought, were able to complete the task satisfactorily, whereas the younger, iconic representers, were not. Bruner and Kenny suggest that the younger children were unable to restructure and transform their original image of the array to enable them to cope with the new situation.

COMPARISONS WITH PIAGET

Bruner's modes of representation have obvious similarities with Piaget's stages of development. However, a major difference arises from Bruner's insistence that, although we acquire these modes sequentially during childhood, the adult retains and uses all three throughout life. We do not 'pass through' the earlier modes, and although adult thinking employs mainly the symbolic mode, we employ enactive and iconic thinking also when the need arises.

Bruner places greater emphasis than does Piaget on the part played by experience. He stresses that cognitive growth is significantly influenced by such variables as culture, family and education.

In contrast with Piaget, Bruner stresses the importance of language to the child's developing thought processes. Children who still depend upon iconic thought are dominated by the images they perceive; their ability to re-structure and reflect upon these images is limited. Parents and teachers should encourage children to describe problems and events by talking and writing about their experiences in order to encourage symbolic rather than iconic representation.

SELF-ASSESSMENT QUESTIONS

1   Briefly describe the three major ways in which, according to Bruner, individuals represent the environment to themselves.

2   Compare Bruner's theory with that of Piaget.

SECTION III:
INFORMATION-PROCESSING APPROACH TO COGNITIVE DEVELOPMENT

This is a relatively new approach to the study of cognitive development which is gathering momentum, particularly in the United States. Information-processing psychologists, while influenced by Piaget, do not subscribe to a single, unified theory in their work. Their aim is to understand how a child interprets, stores, retrieves and evaluates information. This approach includes the following:

1   a detailed study of processes such as perception, memory, the use of strategies, reaction times, the efficiency with which attention can be allocated, and so on;

2   an attempt to understand what aspects of information-processing change with age and which are relatively stable. For example, a child's capacity to handle several items of information at one time increases with age.

The work of Case (1978) exemplifies the information-processing approach. Some of his propositions can be summarised as follows.

1   Cognitive development occurs in a series of ordered stages during which the child's information-processing capacities become increasingly more proficient.

2   The crucial concept in explaining development is the amount of 'working memory' (roughly equivalent to short-term memory) the child possesses at a particular time. Tasks that the child encounters can be described in terms of the amount of working memory or 'M-space' they require. As a child develops, the amount of working memory available increases.

41

"I WAS LIKE YOU — THOUGHT
I KNEW IT ALL — THEN THEY
STARTED ON THINGS CALLED
WORDS ! "

3   If one knows a subject's M-capacity, it is possible to predict her/his performance in a wide range of tasks. Also, the child's performance can be improved by providing memory aids or by reducing the demands made on working memory.

Case's model of cognitive development is extremely complex and, as he himself indicates, remains to be completely worked out.

SELF-ASSESSMENT QUESTIONS

1   How does the information-processing approach to cognitive development differ from that of Piaget?

2   Give a brief account of the work of one psychologist who subscribes to the information-processing approach.

SECTION IV: LANGUAGE ACQUISITION

The basic units of a language are words and each word is made up of sounds, known as **phonemes**, which correspond roughly to the letters of the alphabet. Phonemes combine together to form **morphemes** which are the smallest units of language to have a grammatical purpose. For example, the word 'pins' is made up of four phonemes — p-i-n-s and two morphemes — 'pin', which is a word, and 's' which serves the purpose of converting the word to the plural.

In the remarkably short time span of about three years young children progress from speaking their first word, at approximately 12 months, to producing fluent, grammatically correct speech. Without any deliberate training, children are able to acquire a working knowledge of grammar, or syntax (combining morphemes so that they obey systematic rules) by the time they are about four and a half. At the same time, their understanding of the meaning of words and sentences (semantics) develops rapidly.

Psychologists are interested in a number of questions about language acquisition. They include the following.

1   What accounts for the rapid progress in mastering such a complex and intricate system as language?

2   To what extent does language acquisition depend upon biological factors (nature) and to what extent upon learning (nurture)?

SEQUENCE OF LANGUAGE ACQUISITION

There are three main phases of early language acquisition.

1   **Babbling** — The first sounds a child makes are cries, which reflect

the child's physical state of well-being, followed soon by gurgles, coos and chuckles, which are not, strictly speaking, language, but are thought to represent what Vygotsky called the 'pre-intellectual' stage. At about five or six months the child begins to babble, producing syllable-like sounds, e.g. gaga, dada. All babies, including those who are deaf, produce these same speech-like sounds, indicating that maturation, rather than learning is responsible. Towards the end of the first year the sounds made begin to resemble the language that is spoken around the child.

2   **One-word utterances** — At about 12 months, the child produces her/his first understandable words, e.g. 'Mummy' 'Dog' 'No'. The child's active vocabulary by the age of 18 months is, on average, about 50 words, though she/he will understand and react correctly to many more that she/he cannot yet utter.

3   **Early sentences** — At about the age of two years, children begin to put two words together to form simple sentences, e.g. 'Mummy go', 'Teddy fall'. These words are not randomly linked, but appear to be 'telegraphic' versions of adult sentences, in which essential nouns, verbs and occasional adjectives are uttered (see Roger Brown's work below). From the start, it seems, the child is capable of following simple rules of grammar.

STUDIES OF LANGUAGE ACQUISITION

Trevarthen (1974) studied babies from birth to six months with the aid of recording devices. He noted a particular kind of behaviour in babies as young as six weeks which he termed 'pre-speech'. This is a primitive attempt at speech by moving the lips and tongue, sometimes vocally, at other times soundlessly. He noted also that as early as two months, babies make soft, low vowel sounds in response to others. This responsive vocalisation may be the beginning of 'taking turns' as babies and adults do in conversation later on.

In a longitudinal study lasting 10 years, **Roger Brown** used naturalistic observation techniques to study the development of language in three children, Adam, Eve and Sarah. The children were visited in their homes and tape recordings made of conversations between child and mother. The tape recordings were later transcribed and analysed by Brown and colleagues. The following are among the insights obtained from Brown's work.

1   Early sentences produced by young children are short and incomplete grammatically. However, the words retained are 'telegraphic' in that they preserve the meaning of the message, while the smaller 'functor' words, which are not essential to the meaning,

are left out, e.g. 'baby highchair', meaning 'baby is in the highchair'. Correct word order is invariably retained.

2　Children up to the age of four/five have difficulty in correctly expressing negation (I will **not** walk), past tenses (I shout**ed**), plurals (give me the sweet**s**).

3　Early sentences are much the same whatever language the child speaks. Whether the child is learning English, Russian or Chinese, she/he expresses the same variety of meanings, e.g. statements about location ('spoon table'), possession ('my doll') actions ('Mummy dance').'

Brown's innovatory approach to the study of language acquisition has produced a vast amount of data which has provided material for many further studies. However, the study has its limitations. Because of the nature and size of the sample, it is difficult to generalise findings to all children. Also, child speech was analysed from a typed transcript of the recordings. It was noted by Robinson (1981) that features of the language used, such as intonation, pitch and stress were not included, and the caretaker's utterances and the context in which the utterances were made were often left out.

Cazden (1965) found that a group of children whose utterances were commented upon on a regular basis over a period of three months showed more progress in language development than a similar group whose utterances were expanded upon and imitation of correct language encouraged.

THEORIES OF LANGUAGE ACQUISITION

Learning theory

Learning theorists view reinforcement and imitation as the principal mechanisms governing a child's acquisition of language. Skinner (1957) distinguishes three ways in which speech may be encouraged.

— The child uses **echoic** responses, i.e. imitates sounds made by others, who immediately show approval. In line with the principles of operant conditioning (see Chapter 4), this reinforcement increases the likelihood of the word being repeated on future occasions in the presence of the object.

— The child produces a **mand**, i.e. a random sound, which then has a meaning attached by others; e.g. on hearing 'dada' the parent uses it to form a word and encourages the child to repeat it.

— A **tact** response is made, where the child utters a word, usually imitated, in the presence of the object, and is rewarded by approval.

Gradually, through the processes of imitation, trial and error and reinforcement, the child develops and refines her/his language until it matches that of the parents.

Limitations of the learning theory approach

Learning theory cannot explain:

— the remarkable rate of language acquisition. An impossible number of utterances would need to be imitated/reinforced if these were the only mechanisms responsible;

— the many different responses that may be made to the same verbal stimuli;

— the creative and novel utterances made by children. 'Mouses', 'I seed', 'He goed' — all common childhood utterances — are unlikely to have been acquired though imitation and reinforcement. Herriot (1970) argues that these 'virtuous errors' arise because the child is actively trying to apply 'correct' grammatical rules, and has not had sufficient experience to remember the irregular morphemes.

The learning theory explanation relies heavily on the role of the caretaker in acting as a model for the child's speech and providing reinforcement. However, Brown and others observed that parents rarely correct a child's grammar or reinforce grammatically correct statements. Rather, they tend to be interested in the truth or correctness of the utterances. McNeill (1966) showed that when parents do attempt to correct a child's speech the results are often disappointing, as the following dialogue demonstrates:

Child: Nobody don't like me
Mother: No, say 'nobody likes me'
Child: Nobody don't like me

After eight repetitions:
Child: Oh, nobody don't likes me.

Dodd (1972) studied babies' utterances during the babbling stage and found there was no imitation of sounds made by an attentive adult, though the amount of babbling increased.

Imitation and reinforcement clearly play a part in language acquisition, but learning theory does not appear to provide the whole explanation.

Nativist theory

Chomsky (1968) strongly opposed Skinner's learning theory explanation of language acquisition and stressed the likelihood of some biologically based predisposition to acquire language. He maintained that humans possess an inborn brain mechanism which he terms a **'language**

acquisition device'. The language acquisition device contains certain information about the structure of language which is progressively used as the child matures.

At some level, all languages share common elements. Chomsky calls these common features 'linguistic universals'. One sort of 'universal' relates to the existence of nouns, adjectives and verbs, which are common to all languages. These 'universals' exist at the 'deep' structural level in languages. Through the language acquisition device the child has an innate awareness of these universals. The differences that exist between the various languages, Chomsky suggests, exist at the 'surface' structure.

When a child is exposed to language, she/he is able to 'scan' what is heard, extract the underlying grammatical rules and apply them in new situations and in varying forms (transformations).

Arguments in support of Chomsky's theory include:

—   The existence of 'linguistic universals' must point to an innate capacity for language in humans. Chomsky argues that this predisposition is not shared by other species. However, studies aimed at investigating whether non-human primates can acquire language have cast some doubt on this assertion. (See Gardner & Gardner 1969; Premack 1972.)

—   The fact that children acquire language so competently in such a short time span is quite remarkable, particularly in view of the fragmented and often distorted samples of speech they are exposed to in the home. Such a feat could not be accomplished without the existence of an inborn capacity for language. However, it should be remembered that a child does not acquire language in isolation from the social context in which it occurs. It is likely that speech heard by the child is interpreted in conjunction with its social context.

—   All human beings possess common physiological features related to language, such as finely tuned vocal chords, and language areas in the cortex of the brain. Furthermore, virtually all children, regardless of their intellectual ability, acquire language at approximately the same age and in the same sequence (Lenneberg 1967).

A major criticism of Chomsky's theory has been directed at its concentration on the structure of sentences, while neglecting their meaning. For example, the theory cannot explain single word utterances since they contain no grammatical structure.

SELF-ASSESSMENT QUESTIONS

1   Outline the three main phases of language acquisition in children.

2   Briefly describe a study of language acquisition which used observational techniques. What are the methodological limitations of such a study?

3   Comment upon two distinctive features of the language of children below the age of four/five years.

4   Briefly outline either the learning theory or the nativist approach to language acquisition. What are the 'flaws' in such an approach?

FURTHER READING

Bryant P Piaget: issues and experiments. **British Journal of Psychology**. Special issue. 1982.

De Villiers P A & J G De Villiers **Early language**. Fontana 1979.

Donaldson M **Children's minds**. Fontana 1978.

McGurk H **Growing and Changing** Methuen 1975.

Mussen P, J Conger & A Huston **Child development and personality** (6th Edition). New York Harper & Row 1984.

Turner J **Cognitive development and education** . Methuen 1984.

Chapter 4

Social and Moral Development

At the end of this chapter you should be able to:

1   describe and evaluate psychodynamic, learning theory and cognitive approaches to development;

2   compare and contrast these three developmental approaches;

3   describe psychodynamic, social learning theory and cognitive approaches to moral development;

4   evaluate these approaches in the light of empirical evidence;

5   briefly describe some research into
    (a)   the effects of parental discipline and
    (b)   peer-group influences on moral development.

INTRODUCTION

Three major theoretical approaches have contributed to our knowledge of social and moral behaviour:

1   the psychodynamic approach which arises from Freud's theory of personality development;

2   the learning theory approach, which is based on the work of the early Behaviourists such as Watson, Pavlov and Thorndike, and currently upheld by psychologists such as Skinner and Bandura;

3   the cognitive approach which is derived largely from Piaget's theory of cognitive development.

Each approach will be considered in turn.

SECTION I: PSYCHODYNAMIC APPROACH

INTRODUCTION

Freud's psychoanalytic view of child development has had a profound effect on psychological thinking since its introduction in the early part of this century.

Originally trained as a doctor, Freud's interest in neurology led him to specialise in nervous disorders. He noted that many neurotic disorders exhibited by his patients appeared to stem from former traumatic experiences rather than from physical complaints. Freud gradually developed his now famous psychoanalytic treatment of emotional and personality disorders.

Psychoanalysis involves the use of three major techniques:

1   'free association' — encouraging patients to express the free flow of thoughts entering their minds;

2   analysis of dreams;

3   interpretation of 'slips of speech' and other 'accidental events'.

Each of these techniques, Freud believed, would penetrate the **unconscious mind** of the patient and reveal thoughts, feelings and motivations of which the patient was not consciously aware.

From this early work emerged Freud's monumental theory of the human mind and personality. Central to the theory are his belief in:

—   the importance of early childhood experiences for later personality and emotional development;

—   the existence of the unconscious mind harbouring repressed memories which motivate and influence conscious thoughts and behaviour;

—   the existence of **instinctual drives** which motivate and regulate human behaviour even in childhood. The source of these drives is psychic energy, and the most important, the **libido**, is sexual in nature. Libido is a force which compels humans to behave in ways which are likely to reproduce the species.

—   the importance of **defence mechanisms** such as **repression** (removing painful experiences from conscious memory); **regression** (reverting back to earlier ways of behaving in order to escape from stressful events); **projection** (expressing one's own disturbing feelings or attitudes as though they arose from another person); **sublimation** (expressing basic drives, for example aggressive tendencies, in a substitute activity — such as art).

An important concept introduced by Freud is that of **identification**, a psychological mechanism which aims to explain the increasing similarity between the behaviour of children and older generations.

THE STRUCTURE OF THE PERSONALITY

Freud contends that the personality consists of three major structures —

the id, the ego and the superego. Each structure has its own function and in the healthy, mature personality the three structures produce well-balanced, integrated behaviour.

Id — Freud believed that the child is driven exclusively by the id in early infancy. The id is biologically determined and represents all the instinctual drives that are inherited. It operates on the 'pleasure principle', that is, it seeks immediate gratification of all needs and desires; it is irrational and impulsive and pays no attention to social restrictions.

Ego — As the infant develops and attempts to adapt to the demands of the outside world, the ego develops. It operates on the 'reality principal', its main function being to strike a balance between the inhibitions and constraints of the outside world and the irrational, self-seeking drives of the id. The ego is often said to be the 'executive' or 'manager' of the personality.

Superego — Around the age of four to six, the third structure of the personality, the superego, emerges. Roughly equivalent to the conscience, the superego represents the individual's internal representation of all the moral sanctions and inhibitions which exist in the surrounding culture. Any violation of its often unrealistically high standards results in the individual experiencing guilt and anxiety.

PSYCHOSEXUAL STAGES OF DEVELOPMENT

Freud proposes that in the course of development children pass through a series of stages. During each stage satisfaction is gained as the libido (or sexual energy) is directed towards a different part of the body. The process through which psychic energy is directed towards objects, people or actions is known as **cathexis**. Cathexis reduces drives and attaches energy to objects. Each stage entails a set of problems to be overcome in relation to later development. Failure to negotiate satisfactorily a particular stage, Freud believed, results in **fixation**, or halting of development at that stage, which could, in turn, cause neuroses in adult life.

During the first year of life, the child is said to be in the **Oral Stage**. The id is dominant; libidinal energy is centred on the mouth and the child gains satisfaction from sucking and biting. A child whose oral needs are not satisfied or are over-indulged will exhibit the characteristics of this stage in later life. Fixation may express itself in alcoholism or gluttony or in drug taking and smoking.

During the second or third year of life, libidinal energy shifts from the oral to the anal region of the body. During the **Anal Stage**, the child will gain satisfaction from expelling and with-holding faeces. A significant event in the child's life is the parents' efforts to impose toilet training. Fixation at the anal stage, perhaps resulting from parent/child conflict over toilet training, may give rise to a personality who is exceedingly preoccupied with cleanliness and orderliness (expelling), or who is mean, obstinate and obsessive in adulthood (withholding).

Sometime between the ages of four and six, the child enters the **Phallic Stage**. Now libidinal energy centres on the genitals and feelings become overtly sexual. Describing first the sequence of events for the male child, Freud defined important issues arising from the **Oedipus complex**. The boy's fantasies include wishes for sexual intimacy with his mother. He envies his father's intimate relationship with his mother and fears punishment, in the form of castration, for his forbidden wishes. The Oedipal complex is resolved when the child identifies with his father in order to appease him and to become like him in as many ways as possible.

Freud's account of the progress of female children through the Phallic Stage is less clear cut and he proposed various explanations for the girl's eventual identification with her mother. Possibly the most widely reported — the **Electra complex** — is that the girl, believing herself to be already castrated, since she does not possess a penis, suffers **penis envy**. This leads her to seek a strong love-attachment to her father, the possessor of a penis, and finally to identify with her mother in order to become like her.

The satisfactory resolution of the Oedipus/Electra complex results in the child identifying with the same-sexed parent. Two important conse-quences stem from identification:

— the child adopts the sex-role which will be assumed through life;

— the child adopts the parents' moral standards, attitudes and prohibitions, together with the moral norms of the society they reflect. Thus, the superego, or conscience, is born, and the values and beliefs of a culture are passed on from one generation to the next.

If, through insensitive handling by adults, the child does not satisfactorily overcome the Oedipus/Electra complex, problems lie ahead. Psycho-analysts believe that fixation at the phallic stage lies behind most adult neuroses.

Following the turmoil of the phallic stage, the child enters the calm of the **Latency Period**, which continues until adolescence. During this time the libido is submerged and does not centre upon any bodily area. This is a time of ego-development, particularly in relation to social and intellectual skills.

At adolescence, there is renewed interest in sexual pleasure and the child passes into the final stage of maturity, the **Genital Stage**. All previous sexual drives associated with particular regions of the body come together in an integrated set of adult sexual attitudes and feelings.

EVALUATION

Responses to Freud's theory have varied widely. Many psychologists still vigorously subscribe to his views; some dismiss the theory as being unscientific and not worthy of further study. Yet others, while supporting his central themes, have modified Freud's heavy emphasis on the importance of sexuality. **Erikson** (1963), for example, a neo-Freudian theorist, sees development as largely influenced by social and environmental factors and describes a number of psycho-social stages through which an individual passes during the whole lifespan. (See Chapter 6.)

Eysenck and Wilson (1973) have raised objections to psychoanalytic theory on a number of counts.

— Freud's use of a limited sample of adults, all of whom were emotionally ill in some way, makes it difficult to generalise his theory to all human beings.

— His use of the clinical case study method, unsupported by quantitative data or statistical analysis, makes his theory seem vague and difficult to verify.

— By their very nature, many of the processes described by Freud, for example instinctual drives and defence mechanisms, cannot be directly observed and inferences about human behaviour are often open to alternative explanations. This makes the generation of precise and testable hypotheses difficult. Not only can the theory not be supported, it can not be refuted — a serious violation of the scientific method.

Eysenck and Wilson conclude that psychoanalysis is of historic interest only and has nothing to contribute to our understanding of human behaviour.

Kline (1984), while agreeing that psychoanalytic theory is not scientific, as science is at present conceived, believes that it offers a coherent account of human behaviour in all its complexity. This, he contends, makes it worthy of further scrutiny. Kline argues that while some aspects of the theory, for example instinctual drives, cannot easily be tested and should be abandoned, other aspects can generate testable hypotheses which conform to the demands of the scientific method. He proposes that psychoanalytic theory should be regarded as a collection of hypotheses rather than as one whole theory. These should be restated in a refutable form or, if that is not possible, they should be abandoned. Those that can be tested should then be subjected to an objective, empirical examination.

SOME STUDIES OF FREUD'S IDEAS

Repression: Freud's theory of repression asserts that information which provokes anxiety in the ego can be prevented from entering the consciousness. Many studies have attempted to demonstrate the effects of repression. One study which claims to show how emotional stimuli can influence memory was carried out by Levinger and Clark (1961).

Method: Subjects were shown a list of 60 words one at a time. Half of the words were judged to be emotional (e.g. love, bad, pity) and half 'neutral' (e.g. mouth, sing, lamp). Subjects were asked to free associate (give another word they associated with the stimulus word) to each one. The words were then re-presented and subjects were asked to recall the association words. Immediately after the test, the subjects were again presented with the 60 words and asked to recall their previous association to each one.

Results showed that emotional words produced significantly more forgotten associations than the neutral words. The experimenters concluded that emotional responses are subject to some form of 'emotional inhibition'.

Kline claimed that these findings provide clear evidence of repression operating in memory. However, an alternative explanation offered by Eysenck and Wilson is that the findings support the known relationship between arousal level and memory. The basis of their argument is as follows:

— emotional stimuli are likely to produce a higher level of arousal in the subject than are neutral stimuli;

— highly arousing words are more poorly recalled after short time intervals, but better recalled after longer time intervals;

— it follows that if Levinger and Clark had allowed more time to elapse before subjects were asked to recall the words, the emotional words might have been better recalled than the neutral words.

Parkin, Lewinsohn and Folkard (1982) evaluated these two competing explanations of Levinger and Clark's experiment. The experiment was replicated using two groups of subjects.

Method: The first group were shown the stimulus words and asked to recall the associations immediately. For the other group the procedure was the same except that recall was requested after a time lapse of one week.

Results showed that for the 'immediate recall' group neutral words were better remembered than emotional words. This is in line with Levinger and Clark's findings. For the 'delayed recall' group the reverse was true: emotional words were better recalled than neutral words. (A graphic representation of these findings appears in Figure 6.)

Conclusions: These findings appear to support the arousal theory of memory and offer no support for the Freudian theory of repression. However, an objection to this study and others like it is that the stimuli used may be too trivial and artificial to activate the deep emotional responses described by Freud.

Figure 6

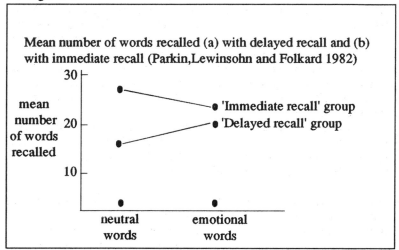

Mean number of words recalled (a) with delayed recall and (b) with immediate recall (Parkin, Lewinsohn and Folkard 1982)

Oral fixation: It could be hypothesized that babies who had been denied adequate oral satisfaction during early feeding would suck their thumbs when older, indicating fixation in the oral stage of development. Yarrow (1973) in a study of 66 children, gathered data on age of weaning, time spent feeding and later incidence of thumb-sucking. No significant correlation was found between age of weaning and later thumb-sucking. However, a significant correlation was found between time spent feeding and later thumb-sucking, those children with the shortest feeding times later being the most persistent thumb-suckers. Some support is claimed for Freud's notion of fixation in the oral stage and its effects on later behaviour. An alternative explanation may be that children whose greater need for sucking, for whatever reason, led them to feed more quickly, and later to satisfy the need through thumb-sucking.

Anal fixation: Freud's theory suggested that over-strict potty training in the anal stage would result in personality traits such as obstinacy, obsessiveness and pre-occupation with cleanliness and orderliness. Kline (1966) correlated two sets of data: scores derived from a measure of the anal personality in the form of a questionnaire; and scores on the anal card of the Blacky Picture Test (a projective test consisting of a number of pictures of a puppy, one of which shows Blacky defaecating between the kennels of his parents). Findings demonstrated a modest correlation between these two scores. Kline believes this offers some support for Freudian theory.

Kline considered that a major difficulty in investigating the anal personality lay in the embarrassment and modesty people in our culture feel in relation to faeces and defaecation, which made it difficult to include direct questions in the questionnaire.

Critics of this study have questioned whether agreement to questions such as 'Do you regard the keeping of dogs as unhygienic?' are really linked to Freudian theory, or simply a reflection of a general concern with cleanliness.

Oedipus/Electra Complex: Friedman (1952) investigated the Oedipus/Electra complex in over 300 children between five and 16 years of age.

Method: The children were shown three pictures: (1) a mother and child; (2) father and mother; and (3) for boys, father and son standing by some stairs near a toy waggon, and for girls, father and daughter by the stairs with a girl doll nearby. Psychoanalytic themes and symbols in the children's responses were analysed.

Findings

1   Both boys and girls produced more conflict themes with the same-sex parent than with the opposite sex parent.

2   More girls than boys fantasized that the father figure took some positive action to the toy.

3   More girls than boys fantasised that the father figure mounted the stairs and entered the room. In Freudian theory, mounting the stairs is symbolic of sexual intercourse.

   All of these sex differences were supported at a high level of statistical significance.

Friedman claims that all of these findings were consistent with Freudian theory and offer support for the Oedipus/Electra complex.

Critics of this study have argued that these findings could be explained quite simply without reference to Freudian theory. For example, the first two findings may simply reflect the tendency in American and British families for girls to argue more with their mothers and boys with their fathers, and that the father is the active decision-maker in many families.

It has also been suggested that projective tests, such as the one used in this study and the Blacky Picture Test, rely too heavily upon the investigator's subjective interpretation of subjects' responses, rather than on more objective criteria.

KLINE'S REVIEW OF EMPIRICAL EVIDENCE

In his review of studies which have attempted to investigate Freudian concepts, Kline (1984) concludes as follows.

—   So far as the Oedipus conflict is concerned, a range of cross-cultural and other studies with children have supported hypotheses derived from Freudian theory (Stephens 1962; Friedman 1952).

- There is only weak evidence to support links between oral and anal personality traits and child-rearing procedures, but no firm support. This, Kline believes, is partly due to the problems involved in carrying out adequate studies.

- There is a degree of empirical support for defence mechanisms and, especially, repression.

Kline stresses that it would be wrong to dismiss Freudian theory as false at this stage of knowledge, and he pleads for bold and original thinking in future attempts to investigate Freudian concepts.

FOOTNOTE

At the current stage of psychological knowledge, there appears to be no indisputable evidence to support Freud's developmental theory. While a considerable amount of empirical support can be found, alternative explanations are often available to account for the findings. Nonetheless, most people would intuitively support many Freudian concepts; for example, few would question the existence of a hidden — or unconscious — part of the mind which sometimes, inexplicably, influences actions and thoughts. Most also would subscribe to the existence of defence mechanisms.

Perhaps the final comment should be a reminder of the immense contribution Freud has made to the study of child development. His emphasis on the importance of early childhood for later personality development and his attempt to account for individual differences in development have stimulated a great deal of research and will undoubtedly continue to do so in the future.

SELF-ASSESSMENT QUESTIONS

1   Explain the terms id, libido and cathexis as used by Freud.

2   Briefly describe the first three psychosexual stages of development, noting the consequences for adult life of fixation in these stages.

3   Discuss the major objections to Freudian theory.

4   Evaluate two studies which have attempted to provide evidence in support of Freud's psychodynamic theory of child development.

5   What difficulties might be encountered by researchers who attempt to study Freudian ideas?

" IT'S REALLY REINFORCING,
SEEING HIM WITH HIS
SUCCESSFUL THEORY ! "

SECTION II: LEARNING THEORY APPROACH

Learning may be defined as a relatively permanent change in behaviour which comes about through experience or practice. Learning theorists are a group of psychologists who believe that socialisation is influenced mainly by external, environmental factors, rather than by factors within the individual. They do not deny that maturation plays a part in development, but rather suggest that the process is of limited value in explaining changes in behaviour.

According to psychologists who subscribe to the learning theory view of development, human beings are quite similar at birth and have the potential to develop into similar adults. However, each individual has varying experiences and receives different treatment from others. Throughout development, these diverse experiences accumulate and result in unique individuals, each with their own typical patterns of behaviour. One person lives in a loving, caring environment, so she develops into a happy, optimistic personality; another lives in a deprived environment where he is mistreated, and he grows up withdrawn and unsociable. According to learning theorists, the same individual may have been totally different had her/his life-experiences taken a different course.

Three theories of learning are used to account for how a child may develop such a complex pattern of behaviours, concepts and habits. Two of these theories are based upon conditioning processes, where new associations are formed between objects and events in the environment and the individual's responses. The third theory postulates changes in behaviour brought about by an individual observing and imitating the behaviour of others.

CLASSICAL CONDITIONING

Reflex behaviour is involuntary; it arises automatically in response to an appropriate stimulus, for example salivating, eye-blinking and emotional reactions such as fear. Classical conditioning aims to account for the way in which reflex behaviour may become associated with a new stimulus that does not naturally activate that behaviour. Put simply, an individual may **learn** to respond in a particular way to a given stimulus.

Pavlov (1927) a physiologist by training, was studying the salivary reflex in dogs when he observed that the dogs salivated not only at the sight and smell of food, a 'natural' response, but also at the sight of the food container alone. Through a series of experiments he demonstrated that dogs could be conditioned to salivate to other 'unnatural' stimuli, such as a buzzer being sounded, provided the stimulus was repeatedly presented at, or slightly before, the presentation of food. Such a pairing caused an association to be formed between the buzzer and the food and subsequently between the buzzer and the salivation response. A **conditioned reflex** had been formed.

Figure 7

THE PROCESS OF CLASSICAL CONDITIONING

Procedure   **Response**

Before Conditioning

Food
(UCS) ——————————→ Salivation
(UCR)

Buzzer
(CS) ——————————→ No response
or irrelevant
response

During Conditioning

Food plus buzzer
(UCS)   (CS) ——————————→ Salivation
(UCR)

Repeated pairing of the UCS and CS

After Conditioning

Buzzer
(CS) ——————————→ Salivation
(CR)

Key:
UCS   = Unconditioned stimulus
CS   = Conditioned stimulus
UCR   = Unconditioned response
CR   = Conditioned response

Figure 7 illustrates the process of classical conditioning and the terminology associated with it.

Pavlov further demonstrated that after conditioning:

1   the dog would **generalise** its response by salivating to sounds similar to the buzzer;

2   if the conditional stimulus continued to be present but without the food, the salivating response would cease, or be **extinguished**;

3   if two different tones were sounded but food was presented with only one of them, the dog would learn to **discriminate** between them and salivate only to the tone associated with food.

Classical conditioning in infants

Pavlov's procedures and terminology were soon applied to experimentation with young children. Watson and Rayner (1920) demonstrated that fear could be developed through classical conditioning and could be eliminated in the same way. Watson proposed that the emotion of fear (UCR) in infants is a natural response to a loud noise (UCS). He produced a fear of rats (and indeed of all white furry things) (CR) in a nine month old baby by repeatedly associating the appearance of a rat (CS) with the sound of a loud gong (UCS).

Learning theorists propose that classical conditioning may be responsible for the development of many irrational fears. For example, the child who undergoes a frightening experience associated with the presence of a dog may develop a long-lasting fear of all dogs.

Marquis (1931) demonstrated the process of classical conditioning in ten new born babies by sounding a buzzer shortly before or at the same time as they received their bottle. After this treatment had continued for eight days, it was noted that the infants made sucking movements and generally increased their activity when the buzzer was presented without the food. Marquis concluded that 'systematic training of the human infant . . . can be started at birth'.

More recently, several experimenters have shown that the heart rates of some two and three day old infants can be altered through classical conditioning procedures.

Studies of classical conditioning have demonstrated the existence of a powerful process capable of influencing reflex behaviour in both animals and human beings.

OPERANT CONDITIONING

Unlike classical conditioning, operant conditioning is concerned with **voluntary** behaviour. This branch of the learning theory tradition is based upon the work of Thorndike (1913), but is currently associated with the name of B F Skinner, the American Behaviourist.

Skinner showed, in a well-known series of laboratory experiments, how animals such as rats could be conditioned to perform pre-specified behaviour such as pressing a lever. He constructed a small box containing a lever, a food dispenser and (sometimes) a panel to display lighted stimuli. A rat placed in the box spontaneously explores its surroundings and eventually, by accident, presses the lever. This activates the food dispenser and a pellet of food is presented to the rat. Subsequently, each time the animal's behaviour approximates to what is required, food is presented, until eventually the 'reward' is produced only when the animal presses the lever. This procedure is known as **behaviour shaping**: the desired behaviour is shaped by rewarding a series of responses that are **successive approximations**. The desirable behaviour, in this case, lever pressing, was named an operant. The reward, which increases the likelihood of the behaviour (or operant) being repeated, is the **reinforcer**.

As with classical conditioning, generalisation, discrimination and extinction can be demonstrated.

1   An animal may **generalise** its response to situations which are similar but not identical to the one in which it was originally conditioned. Therefore, if a rat is conditioned to respond when a one inch plastic square is presented, it will also press the lever in response to a circle of a similar size.

2   The rat may then be conditioned to **discriminate** between the circle and the square if it is reinforced only when it presses the bar in response to one of them, but not the other.

3   If reinforcement is discontinued, **extinction** of the operant response will occur.

Experiments investigating operant conditioning have demonstrated a number of different **schedules of reinforcement**.

1   **Continuous reinforcement** occurs when a reward is given to every instance of the desired behaviour.

2   **Partial reinforcement** may be employed when a rat is reinforced only a proportion of the time at regular intervals.

Partial reinforcement schedules can be operated in four basic ways:

1   Fixed interval: the rat is reinforced after regular time intervals, say every 50 seconds, provided at least one lever pressing response is made during that time.

2   Variable interval: reinforcement is given *on average* every, say, 50 seconds, though not at precisely the same time intervals.

3   Fixed ratio: the rat is reinforced after a regular number of lever pressing responses, say, after every four responses.

4   Variable ratio: Reinforcement is given *on average* every, say, four responses, though not exactly after each fourth response.

Each schedule produces a different kind of learning. In general, continuous reinforcement produces the quickest learning, while partial reinforcement produces learning which lasts longer in the absence of reinforcement. People who regularly seek out the pay phone which occasionally regurgitates money can vouch for the effectiveness of partial reinforcement.

Skinner and others have repeatedly demonstrated that the techniques of operant conditioning can be used to produce extremely complex behaviour in animals. By carefully shaping the component behaviours, he has 'taught' pigeons to act as pilots in rockets and to play table tennis.

Operant conditioning with humans

As with classical conditioning, research has shown that infant behaviour may be shaped through the techniques of operant conditioning.

1   In a study of language acquisition, Rheingold *et al.* (1959) and Bloom (1979) showed that the number of sounds made by three month old babies could be increased by reinforcing the infants' utterances with verbal responses from an adult.

2   Operant methods have also been systematically used in order to change undesirable behaviour in humans (behaviour modification). Efforts to improve the classroom behaviour of disruptive children, to teach basic hygiene routines to the mentally handicapped, to encourage autistic children to communicate, have received some measure of success. In all cases, the techniques used operate on the basis of ignoring undesirable behaviour, resulting in its extinction, and reinforcing desirable behaviour, which should then be repeated.

PUNISHMENT

Punishment is also a concept which is employed by learning theorists. Punishment can be defined as the delivery of an unpleasant stimulus following a response. Just as reinforcement can be used to strengthen the preceding response, making it more likely to be repeated, so punishment can weaken the response and make it less likely to recur.

Whether or not punishment is effective with children is a vexed question. Studies have shown that in the short term it appears to suppress undesirable behaviour. It can, however, have unintended emotional effects such as anger and frustration, and, in some circumstances, it may actually become reinforcing, as in the case of the child whose tantrums are designed to gain attention. In these circumstances it may increase, rather than suppress, the unwanted behaviour.

SOCIAL LEARNING THEORY

Theorists who have attempted to use the insights derived from classical and operant conditioning to account for the development of complex human social behaviours have experienced some difficulties. Critics have questioned the validity of extrapolating the findings of animal experiments to human behaviour and have also raised doubts as to the likelihood of all complex human behaviour being derived from reinforcement of the spontaneous responses of the young child. The concept of observational learning (or imitation) had been proposed to explain language acquisition during early childhood and seemed appropriate also to the acquisition of social behaviour. The scope of learning theory was therefore enlarged to include the process of observational learning (or modelling) to explain how children may learn new behaviour by imitating another person.

Observational learning

Observational learning has been extensively studied by **Bandura** and his colleagues (1963, 1977). A long series of experiments was carried out, mainly using nursery school children as subjects.

In his most famous studies Bandura exposed groups of children to either a real-life situation or to a film in which a model knocked down and beat a rubber 'Bobo' doll. The children were then given the opportunity to reproduce the behaviour observed and their responses were compared to those of a control group who had not seen the model. Findings indicated that the children behaved more aggressively than did the control group, and also reproduced many of the specific acts of the model.

In a later study Bandura showed that children may learn the behaviour of a model without necessarily reproducing that behaviour. Three groups of children were shown a film of a model behaving aggressively; one group saw the model punished for the behaviour, one saw the model rewarded, and the third group observed neither reward or punishment. Subsequent observation of the children's behaviour revealed different levels of imitation. The 'model punished' group reproduced less aggressive behaviour than did the other two groups. Bandura concluded that vicarious punishment (experiencing the model's punishment as though it were administered to oneself) had influenced the children's learning of the aggressive behaviour. However, when the children were then offered rewards for imitating the model's behaviour, all three groups produced equally aggressive behaviour. It is therefore necessary to distinguish between **acquisition** of behaviour, and the **performance** of that behaviour.

Bandura and others went on to investigate what characteristics of a model were most likely to encourage imitation in children. Studies have shown that children are more likely to perform behaviour imitated from models who are:

- similar in some respects to themselves;
- exhibit power and control over some desirable commodity;
- are seen to be rewarded for their actions;
- are warm and nurturant.

Bandura proposes that the ability to observe and then reproduce behaviour involves at least four skills:

1   observation of appropriate and distinctive features of the behaviour;

2   retention of the critical features of the performance;

3   adequate duplication of the model;

4   justification of imitation in terms of internal, external or vicarious rewards.

These processes are evident, he contends, in all manner of modelling, from the imitation of single acts to the reproduction of complex social behaviour. For example, in Bandura's view, gender-role identity (see Chapter 5) arises from repeatedly observing appropriate models.

Identification is a concept derived originally from psychoanalysis and introduced by Freud. It is the process through which a child adopts the feelings, attitudes and behaviour of other people, initially the parents. Identification is similar to imitation in that it involves the child copying the behaviour of others, though it is a more subtle and long-term process. Most psychologists view identification as a fundamental process in the socialisation of the child. Each child identifies to some extent with both parents and as she/he grows older, with other family members and with peers and adults outside the family.

EVALUATION OF THE LEARNING THEORY VIEW OF DEVELOPMENT

- The learning theorists aim to account for all behaviour changes in human beings, including those which occur during development. So far as classical and operant conditioning processes are concerned, numerous studies have shown beyond doubt that the behaviour of young children can be conditioned by both methods. However, critics question whether these studies, most of which have been concerned with controlled, laboratory-based situations, have really addressed the question of how conditioning affects development.

- The question is asked, also, whether behaviour that must be continuously reinforced resembles that which develops naturally and continues to be exhibited without regular reinforcement. The literature on conditioning lacks clear notions of when and why certain kinds of conditioning are possible and what responses are suitable for conditioning at different points in development.

— Studies of learning by observation, with their emphasis on modelling in children of different ages and in a variety of situations, appear to provide a more coherent view of the role of learning in development. However, this approach too often suffers from the limitations inherent in attempting to telescope the whole socialisation process into a single, usually laboratory-based, situation.

— Whatever the role of learning in development, it is clear that other factors also play a part. Learning theorists do not address themselves to the role of biological factors in the developmental process.

— Learning theorists view the child as continually changing as a result of conditioning and imitation of models. This view implies that the child is a passive being who is capable only of responding to external influences. Other theorists, of whom the most notable is Piaget, emphasise the child's active role in her/his own development.

— Perhaps the main limitation of the learning theory approach to human development is its failure to explain spontaneous changes in behaviour that can not easily be accounted for by either conditioning or modelling, for example the emergence of a novel or creative idea or the unexpected solving of a problem.

SELF-ASSESSMENT QUESTIONS

1   What do you understand by 'the learning theory' approach to development? Give details of three types of learning which learning theorists consider to be involved in the developmental process.

2   How might learning theorists explain the development of a phobia, or irrational fear?

3   What is meant by behaviour shaping? Briefly describe an instance of the use of behaviour shaping techniques to condition animal behaviour.

4   Briefly describe an early study which illustrates Bandura's approach to the study of observational learning in children.

5   Briefly describe and discuss the implications of a study which distinguished between the acquisition of behaviour and the manifestation (or performance) of that behaviour.

6   What do you understand by identification? What is its role in the socialisation process?

7   Briefly evaluate the learning theory approach to human development.

SECTION III: COGNITIVE APPROACH: SOCIAL COGNITION

The cognitive approach emphasises that social and emotional behaviour in children is influenced by the way they think and reason at a particular stage of development. Traditionally, this approach has centred upon Piaget's theory of cognitive development. (See Chapter 3 Section I.)

Piaget believed that children's moral and social functioning was closely linked to their stage of cognitive development. The next section in this chapter contains an account of Piaget's views on the ways in which children's cognitive level influences the way they think about moral situations. In the same section is a discussion of the theory of Lawrence Kohlberg, who developed and expanded upon Piaget's account of moral development.

Researchers have, more recently, built upon Piaget's theme and extended it to other areas of social development. A relatively new term has entered the psychological literature, that of social cognition.

SOCIAL COGNITION

Social cognition refers to perception, thinking and reasoning about human beings and about social relationships. Over the past decade or so, developmental psychologists have addressed a number of questions in the area of social cognition. These include the following.

1   How do children understand and conceptualise the social world — the people around them, relationships between themselves and others?

2   What changes take place in such reasoning and concepts as children develop?

3   What is the relationship between cognition and social behaviour?

The following areas are among those that have been studied:

1   children's perceptions of themselves;

2   conceptions of relationships between themselves and other people, for example, authority relations, friendships (see Chapter 5, section IV);

3   moral reasoning.

Basic principles

As noted earlier, a great deal of the research on social cognition has been strongly influenced by Piaget's work. Therefore, many of the underlying principles have been based upon his theory. For example:

1   **Stages of development** — Children's social thinking and reasoning develop through a sequence of stages. All children pass through these stages in the same order and at approximately the same age. Each new stage incorporates and builds upon the characteristics of preceding stages.

2   **Developing thought processes** — Various features of children's thought processes at different stages of development have an effect on how they perceive and understand social situations. As a child develops, thought processes change:

(a)   from simple to complex, that is from their tendency to focus on only one feature of a situation or problem to their ability to take account of many considerations at one time;

(b)   from concrete thinking (where reasoning must be linked to something concrete) to abstract thinking (the ability to think and reason in one's head);

(c)   from rigid to flexible thinking.

These ways of thinking affect a child's understanding of social situations and relationships.

3   **Taking someone else's perspective** — Piaget considered that children below the age of about six or seven are **egocentric**. He believed, therefore, that they are unable to view a problem or a situation from the point of view of another person. As noted in Chapter 3, more recent studies indicate that very young children may not be so egocentric as Piaget believed. Nonetheless, it is clear that the ability to take someone else's perspective (sometimes called role-taking ability) becomes more skilful and sophisticated as a child develops. This ability influences the way the child perceives and reacts to social situations.

Methods of study

While experimental methods have been used to study social cognition, these have often appeared unduly constraining and unrealistic in the context of children's social understanding and behaviour. More often, variations on Piaget's clinical interview method have been used. Typically, a child is told a story about an imaginary social or moral situation. The interviewer then attempts to elicit the child's understanding of the motives and behaviour of characters in the story. Examples of this approach can be seen in Kohlberg's work on moral reasoning and Selman's work on perspective taking and friendships in children.

FOOTNOTE

As research into social cognition has only begun to accumulate during the last 10 years or so, many issues remain to be resolved. For instance, what is the precise relationship between social cognition and other areas of cognition? The classic cognitive approach suggests that cognition develops first in relation to physical objects and only later in relation to social or moral situations. Damon (1977) suggests that there is no reason to assume that one precedes the other. There are some situations, he believes, where social interactions with peers may enhance intellectual functioning, rather than the other way round.

SELF-ASSESSMENT QUESTIONS

1   Outline the traditional cognitive approach to the development of social behaviour.

2   What do you understand by 'social cognition'?

3   In what ways have researchers into social cognition been influenced by Piaget's theory of cognitive development?

4   What problems might arise in using interview methods of study with young children? (See Chapter 1.)

WHICH APPROACH TO DEVELOPMENT?

Three major developmental approaches have been discussed. There are a number of fundamental differences between them. For example:

1   **Active-v-passive nature of the child** - Psychodynamic and learning theorists view the child as largely passive, at the mercy of inner drives (in the former case) and the influence of the environment (in the latter case). Cognitive theorists stress the active, problem-solving nature of the child.

2   **Direction of development** — The basic assumption of both the psychodynamic and cognitive approaches is that development is directional. This implies that the child advances and improves as she/he moves from infancy to maturity. The mature behaviour of the adult is seen as the ideal goal of development. In contrast, learning theorists make no assumptions about the direction of development or the value of the changes that occur.

3   **Biological Influences** — Both Piaget and Freud see development as being influenced by biological changes. In contrast, learning theorists emphasise environmental influences and the role of conditioning and observational learning.

The three approaches arise from theories which focus on different facets of behaviour and make different assumptions about the nature of development. Each has its strengths and weaknesses and each makes an important contribution to our understanding of child development. The goal of developmental psychologists is to move ultimately towards a single, integrated theory which will explain all aspects of psychological development.

SECTION IV: MORAL DEVELOPMENT

The study of moral development has been a topic of research in psychology for over 60 years. An investigation of how a child develops moral values involves looking at the processes through which the child adopts and internalises the rules and standards of behaviour that are expected in the society that she/he grows up in. **Internalisation** may be defined as the process through which standards and values become a part of one's own motive system and guide behaviour, even in the absence of pressure from others.

The major theories that have arisen from the study of moral development fall into three main categories:

1   the psychodynamic approach arising from Freud's theory;

2   the social learning view which draws on the work of Skinner and Bandura; and

3   the cognitive approach characterised by the theories of Piaget and Kohlberg.

Each of these approaches focuses on a particular aspect of the child's experiences and largely ignores other important considerations. For example, Freud's theory emphasises the emotional aspects of moral development, whereas the accounts of Piaget and Kohlberg stress the links between the child's level of moral reasoning and her/his stage of cognitive development. Learning theorists emphasise the role of reinforcement, punishment and observational learning.

Each of these three theories will be discussed, together with a brief account of research into child-rearing styles and peer-group influence.

PSYCHODYNAMIC APPROACH

The first complete theory of moral internalisation was Freud's. The central thrust of the theory, which is concerned with the development of the superego or moral arm of the personality, is as follows.

During the **phallic stage** of psychosexual development (see the account of Freud's theory in Section I of this chapter), the boy encounters the **Oedipus complex**. Overwhelmed by feelings of love for his mother and

70

fear of retaliation from his father, the boy identifies with his father. This involves the child taking over all his father's beliefs, values and attitudes, and through his father, the moral standards and values of the culture he is growing up in. Thus the **superego** is born.

A similar process exists for a girl as she encounters the Electra complex. Freud, however, though aware that the theory was less well-defined for girls than for boys, believed that females develop a weaker superego and consequently are less moral than men. This has, not unexpectedly, angered modern-day feminists.

The superego

The superego, which is unconscious, consists of two distinct parts: the **ego-ideal** and the **conscience**. The ego-ideal is concerned with what is right and proper. It represents the child's image of the sort of virtuous behaviour the parents would approve of. The conscience, on the other hand, watches over what is bad. It intercepts and censors immoral impulses from the id and prevents them from entering the consciousness of the ego.

The superego, then, represents the child's internalisation of rules and prohibitions, initially imposed by the parents, but later adopted by the child in the form of self-discipline independent of parental approval or displeasure. Thus the child becomes capable of controlling her/his own behaviour and preventing him/herself from indulging in the sorts of behaviour forbidden by her/his parents. Transgression of moral rules is likely to be followed by feelings of guilt and anxiety.

Psychodynamic theory predicts that the individual with a strong superego is likely to experience greater feelings of guilt in a situation involving a moral dilemma than does the individual with a weaker superego, and is therefore less likely to transgress the rules. This theory is widely accepted by psychoanalytic theorists, with minor variations, although its main support comes from scattered observations of adult patients (Hoffman 1984). However, Hoffman questions whether a largely unconscious, internalised control system can account for all the complexities of moral behaviour. Other researchers have suggested that, although the superego persists during childhood, it is disrupted in adolescence by hormonal changes, social demands and new information about the world that may contradict it (Erikson 1970).

SOCIAL LEARNING APPROACH

Social learning theorists typically avoid terms such as 'moral internalisation' and concern themselves solely with observable behaviour. However, in attempting to explain moral behaviour, they do describe a similar phenomenon: the individual's ability to behave in a

71

moral way, or refrain from violating moral rules in conditions of temptation, even when no other person is present.

Social learning theory states that initially a child's behaviour is controlled by rewards and punishments from the parents. Because of a history of experiences where a child is punished for transgressing the rules, painful anxiety states become associated with these transgressions. Such anxiety will subsequently be experienced whenever the rules are broken, or in situations involving temptation to behave immorally, even if no other person is present. This explanation has much in common with the concept of the superego.

Bandura's work on observational learning also contributes to the social learning view of moral development. It is assumed that one way children learn moral behaviour is by observing and emulating models who behave in a moral way. Observation of models who are punished for immoral behaviour is said to cause the child to experience vicarious punishment, resulting in the child avoiding that behaviour.

A great deal of research has been inspired by social learning theory, but much of it has serious drawbacks. Perhaps the biggest shortcoming arises from the frequent use of controlled experiments in which a single adult-child interaction is used to indicate the presence or absence of moral behaviour in the child. Such a situation cannot adequately reflect the complexities of the 'real life' socialisation process.

A study by Bandura and MacDonald (1963) which claims support for the social learning view will be discussed later in this chapter.

COGNITIVE APPROACH

Piaget emphasised the cognitive aspect of moral development, believing that a child's moral thinking is linked to her/his stage of cognitive development. Using his own type of clinical methodology, Piaget investigated children's attitudes to **rules** in the game of marbles and their responses to **right and wrong** and **judgement**, as depicted in a series of short stories. A well known example of the latter is the story where children are asked to judge who is naughtier, a boy who accidentally breaks several cups or a boy who breaks one cup while trying to steal jam from the cupboard.

After analysing the responses of numerous children of varying stages of cognitive levels, Piaget concluded that there are two broad stages of moral thinking.

1   The stage of **heteronomous morality** or **moral realism**: in this stage, the child complies strictly with rules, which are viewed as sacred and unalterable. Right and wrong are seen in 'black and white' terms and a particular act is judged on the size of its **consequences**, rather than the intentions of the actor. Thus, the

child who broke several cups is 'naughtier' than the child who broke only one cup, irrespective of the intentions involved.

2   The shift to the second stage, referred to as **autonomous morality**, or **moral relativism**, occurs around the age of seven or eight. Rules are viewed as established and maintained through negotiation and agreement within the social group. Judgements of right and wrong are based on **intentions** as well as consequences. Hence the child who broke a cup in the course of stealing is seen as committing the more serious offence.

Piaget believed that both cognitive development (and therefore maturation) and social experience, particularly interactions with the peer group, play a role in the transformation from one stage to the next. In the earlier, heteronomous stage, the child's moral reasoning is influenced by (a) egocentricity (inability to view events from the point of view of others), and (b) dependence on the authority of adults.

Cognitive-v-social learning theory

A basic objection was raised to Piaget's cognitive theory of moral development by Bandura and McDonald (1963) who doubted the relevance of concepts such as 'stages of development'. In an attempt to explain children's moral judgements through social learning theory they carried out the following experiment.

Groups of children, all of whom had previously taken Piagetian-style tests of moral reasoning, were exposed to a number of conditions in which adult models responded in various ways to similar dilemmas. Results showed that, in general, children imitated their model's responses, even where these responses conflicted with their own usual style of reasoning, as revealed by the earlier Piagetian test. These findings presented a strong challenge to the cognitive approach, which predicts that:

(a)   children at a particular stage of development would be unlikely to imitate responses which conflicted with their level of moral reasoning, and

(b)   children in a higher stage of development would be unlikely to revert to a lower level of moral reasoning.

Critics of the study have commented on the deficiencies of the experimental design and report, and on Bandura and McDonald's failure to pay attention to children's reasons for their judgements.

Langer (1975), in a replication of the experiment, found that:

1   the moral judgements of half the children remained the same even after viewing the model,

2   where children's choices did change, the explanations they gave did not.

Langer concluded that the techniques used in Bandura and McDonald's experiment confused the children, resulting in imitation of the model without true understanding of the reason for the judgement. Hoffman (1979) suggests that children did not merely imitate the model. They were aware that moral acts may or may not be intentional, but placed less emphasis on intentions because the stories used, like Piaget's, portrayed more serious consequences for accidental rather than intended acts. Perhaps if consequences for accidental and intended acts had been equal the children's responses would have been different.

Kohlberg's universal stage model

Building upon Piaget's work, Kohlberg (1969, 1976) attempted to produce a more detailed and comprehensive account of moral development. Like Piaget, Kohlberg focused on an individual's reasoning when presented with a series of moral dilemmas in the form of short stories. Kohlberg's 'moral stories' have been presented to thousands of people of all ages, intelligence levels and socio-economic backgrounds.

Kohlberg sees moral development as occurring at three levels, each of which contains two distinct stages. Figure 8 gives a brief description of the six stages. He states that these stages are fixed and that everyone passes through them in the same order, starting at the lowest level. The end product of progression through these stages is a mature and reasoned sense of justice.

While the ages at which people attain different levels varies, subjects' responses to Kohlberg's moral dilemmas indicate that, in general, children in middle childhood are pre-conventional (level 1), younger adolescents (13-16 years) are at the conventional level (level 2), and about half of older adolescents (16-20 years) attain the principled level (level 3). Cross-cultural studies have revealed that the same sequence of stages exists in certain other cultures (Kohlberg 1969).

Many studies have provided supporting evidence of the links between children's moral reasoning and their stage of cognitive development. However, Kohlberg's theory has also generated much controversy. Debate centres on the main tenets of Kohlberg's theory:

1   moral reasoning is linked to cognitive development;

2   the stage sequence is the same for everyone —

and on the relationship between Kohlberg's stages and moral *behaviour*. A brief discussion of some relevant research follows.

Research into Kohlberg's theory

—   Rest (1983) has reviewed a dozen cross-sectional and longitudinal studies and reports that subjects do develop moral reasoning in the direction postulated by Kohlberg's theory. However, many subjects

Figure 8

KOHLBERG'S SIX STAGES OF MORAL DEVELOPMENT

LEVEL I - PRECONVENTIONAL   **(Middle Childhood)**

Stage 1: Punishment and obedience orientation

Rules are kept in order that punishment may be avoided. The consequences of an action determine the extent to which that action is good or bad.
The interests and points of view of others are not considered, i.e. the child is egocentric.

Stage 2: Instrumental relativist orientation

A 'right' action is one which is favourable to oneself rather than to others. Some consideration is given to the needs of others, but only where the result is favourable to oneself.

LEVEL II - CONVENTIONAL   **(Approximate age - 13-16 years)**

Stage 3: 'Good boy/girl' orientaton

An action is judged as right or wrong according to the intentions of the actor. Socially acceptable standards of behaviour are valued and 'being good' is important.

Stage 4: 'Law and order' orientation

There emerges a profound respect for authority and a belief that society's rules must be kept.
Consideration is given to the point of view of the system which makes the rules, in addition to the motives of the individual.

Figure 8 (continued)

Level III POST-CONVENTIONAL or PRINCIPLED	
	(Approximate age - 16-20)
Stage 5: Social-contract legalistic orientation	What is right is judged in relation to the majority opinion within a particular society. "The greatest good for the greatest number" is the general rule. It is recognised that moral and legal points of view sometimes conflict with each other.
Stage 6: Universal principles of conscience	Self- chosen ethical principles now dictate one's actions: the equality of human rights and respect for the dignity of human beings as individuals are of paramount importance. When laws conflict with these principles, one acts in accordance with the principle.

show no improvement in moral reasoning over time and one in 14 subjects who are in school actually move back to an earlier stage. In a strict interpretation of stage theory, subjects should continue to move to higher stages, and regression to an earlier stage should not occur.

— Principled reasoning (Level 3) has not been found at all in some groups. Moran and Joniak (1979) have shown that scores on moral judgement tests are closely linked to the sophistication of language used. Therefore, those people whose command of language, particularly the use of abstract terms, is poor may be wrongly judged to be operating at a lower stage of moral reasoning than they are actually capable of.

— Kohlberg claims that the six stages of moral reasoning exist in all cultures. However, Gardner (1982) questions whether it is appropriate to apply Kohlberg's approach to other cultures. Moral judgements in other cultures may be based on very different values and priorities from those in Western cultures. Also, Gardner doubts whether Kohlberg has devised a culturally unbiased measure of moral reasoning.

— A major criticism of Kohlberg's work concerns the extent to which there is a positive relationship between moral reasoning and moral behaviour. Alston (1971) points out that how an individual reasons about moral judgements is less important than how that individual actually behaves when faced with a moral dilemma. In general, there is evidence of a positive relationship between the two (Rest 1983) though it is not a strong one. In one study (Milgram 1974) subjects were led to believe that they were administering severe shocks to another person. Those subjects who refused to administer shocks when instructed to do so by an authority figure were more likely to be at the principled stage of moral development than were subjects who did administer shocks. However, these findings may be the result of other factors not examined in the study, such as intelligence level or naivety concerning psychological experiments.

CHILD-REARING PRACTICES

There is a large body of research which suggests that the type of parental discipline administered in childhood affects moral development. In a review of the research Hoffman draws attention to two contrasting styles of discipline used by parents:

1   the use of 'inductions', that is discipline techniques which encourage the child to reflect on her/his behaviour and consider the effects of wrong-doing on other people;

2   'power assertive' discipline, which involves the use of force, threats and withdrawal of privileges.

The central finding is that the frequent use of inductions fosters a personality who behaves morally even when there is no pressure from others to do so, and who is likely to experience strong guilt feelings when she/he does transgress. In contrast, the use of power assertive techniques by parents is associated with individuals who behave morally solely to avoid punishment.

It has been pointed out that most of the studies are correlational, and therefore prevent inferences about a causal link (see Chapter 1) between type of discipline and moral internalisation. However, Hoffman argues that the weight of evidence is such that it must be assumed that style of parental discipline does strongly influence moral development.

PEER INFLUENCES

Despite its undoubted importance, there has been little research on how interaction with peers affects a child's moral development. Correlational studies have shown a negative relationship between early comfortable and frequent interactions with peers and rates of delinquency during adolescence (Conger and Miller 1966).

Experimental research reviewed by Hoffman indicates that if a child observes a peer who behaves aggressively and is not punished, there is an increased likelihood of that child also behaving aggressively.

The role of peers in moral socialisation, and the influence of school experiences (an area which has been neglected), await further research.

SELF-ASSESSMENT QUESTIONS

1   What do psychologists mean by 'moral internalisation'?

2   In what way is the social learning view of moral development similar to Freud's account of the development of the superego? Give one important difference.

3   According to Piaget, what would be the main differences in moral reasoning between a five year old child and a nine year old child?

4   Briefly discuss two similarities between the work of Piaget and that of Kohlberg in the area of moral development.

5   Briefly evaluate Kohlberg's theory.

6   What is the central finding from research into parental discipline and moral development?

FURTHER READING

Eysenck H & G D Wilson **The experimental study of Freudian theories**. Methuen 1973.

Kline P **Psychology and Freudian theory: An introduction**. Methuen 1984.

Mussen P, J Conger & A Huston **Child development and personality** (6th Edition). New York Harper & Row 1984.

McGurk H **Growing and changing**. Methuen 1975.

Chapter 5

Products of Socialisation

At the end of this chapter, you should be able to:

1   describe and assess the findings from research into gender role development.;

2   evaluate alternative explanations of the origins of gender role behaviour;

3   discuss the findings from studies of the emergence of a sense of self in young children;

4   evaluate research into the development of self-esteem in children, and consider some practical implications of research findings;

5   understand what is meant by achievement-motivation and learned helplessness, and assess the practical implications of research into these two constructs.

SECTION I: GENDER

The study of how individuals develop a gender role (or sex role) has been a central concern of developmental psychologists for many years. Gender role development has been an important focus of debate within the major theories of psychology, and is a frequent target of the nature-nurture controversy.

The study of gender role development is beset by a proliferation of similar, often confusing terms. 'Sex' and 'gender' are defined in many dictionaries as synonymous and are often used as such. Thus, different researchers may refer to 'sex-role' or 'gender role' and mean essentially the same thing. Because the term 'sex' has a number of meanings and is usually associated with biological/genital differences, there has been a trend towards using 'gender' to refer to the psychological/cultural aspects of maleness and femaleness. (Huston 1983, has produced a detailed account of sex role taxonomies and definitions.)

MASCULINITY AND FEMININITY

Throughout history, men and women have been perceived as psychologically different in many important ways. These differences have usually been accepted as 'natural' and closely linked to the roles played by the sexes in society. Over the last two decades, however, following the emergence of the women's liberation movement, a great deal of research has raised doubts about the 'natural' nature of these differences and has questioned why it is that women's roles are typically of lower status than those of men.

Research into differences between the sexes has generally posed one of two types of question: firstly, what characteristics do typical males and females possess and how do they differ? Secondly, to what extent do individuals perceive themselves to be masculine or feminine? The first question deals with sex-stereotypes. The second deals with gender-identity.

1   **Sex-stereotypes** — Numerous studies have identified characteristics which can be said to form stereotypes of males and females and there appears to be strong agreement between them. Thus, the typical male is usually seen as assertive, independent, relatively aggressive, good at maths and science; the typical female is dependent, relatively passive, emotional and good at verbal tasks. A study by Ruble (1983) suggests that stereotypes of males and females have changed little in the last 20 years.

2   **Gender-identity** — Early research into self-perceptions of masculinity and femininity tended to place a high value on sex-typing. An important aim of the research was to find ways of helping males and females to acquire appropriate sex-typed attitudes and behaviour in the interests of psychological well being. Masculinity and femininity were seen as representing opposite ends of a continuum, and it was assumed that an individual would exhibit either masculine characteristics or feminine characteristics, but not both.

More recently, Bem (1974) and others have criticised this bi-polar approach, claiming that both so-called masculine and feminine characteristics may develop in the same individual. Thus, a person may be both assertive and warm and still function effectively. Bem has used the term **'androgynous'** to describe people who possess both masculine and feminine characteristics.

Recent studies of gender-identity have attempted to determine whether androgynous individuals are more psychologically healthy and well-adjusted than are individuals who are rigidly typed as either masculine or feminine. Most research has confirmed that this is in fact the case. For example, several studies have reported that androgynous individuals score higher on measures of self-esteem than do individuals who are rigidly sex-typed (Bem 1975, 1983) However, several researchers have suggested that masculine characteristics tend to be more highly valued in western societies, and it may be mainly the masculine aspects of an androgynous personality that are positively related to flexibility and adjustment.

SEX DIFFERENCES IN BEHAVIOUR

Many studies have attempted to discover whether commonly held beliefs about the characteristics of men and women are borne out by the way in which people actually behave. A comprehensive review of the literature was published by Maccoby and Jacklin in 1974. They investigated over 2000 studies of sex differences in personality or intellectual abilities, comparing studies which reported statistically significant sex differences with studies which did not find statistically significant differences. Maccoby and Jacklin reported the existence of sex differences in only four areas: aggressive behaviour and mathematical, spatial and verbal abilities. Specifically, they observed:

(a)   from the age of around 10 or 11, girls score higher than boys on tests of verbal ability, whereas boys perform better on mathematical and spatial tasks;

(b)   boys are more physically aggressive than girls. This difference is evident at all ages from about two years on, and across different cultures.

In other areas where sex differences have been claimed, Maccoby and Jacklin could find no reliable supporting evidence.

A number of controversial problems arise from Maccoby and Jacklin's findings.

1   Some of the studies reviewed are methodologically weaker than others, employing smaller sample sizes and less powerful statistical analyses. Such studies are less likely to find true sex differences. Maccoby and Jacklin's approach in giving each study equal weight could lead to an *under*-representation of true sex differences.

2   Studies which do detect sex differences are more likely to be published. An *over*-representation of sex differences could be present in Maccoby and Jacklin's review.

3   The way studies were categorised may have obscured sex differences. For example, broad categories such as 'social sensitivity' may include characteristics such as role-taking, nurturance and empathy. So, for example, a large number of studies with a 'no differences' finding in role-taking might obscure a true difference in, say, nurturance or empathy.

More recent reviews of sex differences have attempted to avoid some of the methodological problems found in Maccoby and Jacklin's study. In

"THIS IS GOING TO LOOK GOOD ON MY C.V. FOR THE CONSTRUCTION ENGINEERING JOB!"

general, such studies report few strong differences between the sexes (Eisenberg & Lennon 1983).

On the basis of current evidence, little justification can be found for existing sex-stereotypes. So why has there been so much empirical and theoretical attention given to the development of gender-roles and gender-identity? One reason is that whether or not basic characteristics of males and females are similar, their roles in society are very different. In general, adult men and women have very different roles and responsibilities in the home, and in the workplace they operate in very different fields of activity. Women represent the majority of secretaries and nurses, while men account for almost all engineers and mechanics.

As early as two or three, boys can be observed playing in different ways to girls: boys are more likely to play with construction toys and engage in considerable 'rough and tumble' activities; girls are more likely to be found playing with dolls or household toys. By adolescence, distinctive roles are established both in behaviour and in interests and occupational choices.

Thus, differentiation between the sexes is pervasive, and the study of developmental processes can help us understand why. A related concern is an understanding of those processes which may lead to atypical development, such as transsexualism.

FACTORS WHICH INFLUENCE GENDER ROLE DEVELOPMENT

Biological factors

That biology is involved in physical sex differences is, of course, indisputable. The presence of a Y chromosome leads the embryo to develop testes; the absence of the Y chromosome results in the development of ovaries. Hormones affect pre-natal sex differences in anatomy and brain differentiation. The question arises as to what extent these obvious biological differences also extend to psychological development. This question has been addressed in a number of different ways.

Cross-cultural studies — The underlying rationale of this approach is that the sex differences which exist in many different cultures ought to imply that there is a biological basis. In nearly all cultures women are the main caretakers, while men are the warriors and protectors. There is evidence, too, of consistent sex differences across cultures in characteristics such as dominance, aggression and interest in infants. Though these findings suggest biological influences, caution must be exercised in drawing firm conclusions. Cross-cultural similarities in sex roles might be explained by similarities in socialisation practices across different cultures. Also, there are some notable examples of differences between cultures.

Probably the best known example of differences in sex role development between cultures is Margaret Mead's study of three primitive tribes in New Guinea (1935). In the **Arapesh** tribe, both males and females exhibited gentle non-aggressive, affectionate characteristics, behaving in ways traditionally associated with femininity in Western cultures. Among the **Mundugumor** tribe, both males and females behaved in what we would call a 'masculine' way — aggressive and assertive. The **Tchambuli** tribe completely reversed sex roles as we know them. Women were assertive, made decisions about the economic organisation of the tribe and looked after the collection of food; men, on the other hand, took few decisions and spent a lot of time following artistic pursuits.

Mead concluded that sex roles are culturally, rather than biologically, determined. However, Mead has been accused of exaggerating the differences between the Arapesh and Mundugumor tribes. Also, in a later book she adopted the view that there were 'natural' differences between males and females, females being more nurturing and intuitive than males.

Despite the lack of firm evidence from cross-cultural studies, a suggestion does exist of consistent sex differences in aggression and parenting which may result from biological influences, possibly combined with socialisation.

Hormonal influences — Numerous animal studies have provided evidence of the effects of hormones on behaviour. Typically, male and female rats are injected with hormones appropriate to the opposite sex during a sensitive period early in development. Such animals later exhibit behaviour characteristic of the opposite sex. Behaviour studied includes aggression, parenting, rough and tumble play and mating behaviour. These findings suggest that hormonal influences in non-human mammals are responsible for the animals behaving in a masculine or feminine manner. However, the effects of hormone manipulations may vary from species to species, and how relevant such findings are to the understanding of sex differences in humans remains a matter for debate.

For obvious ethical reasons, it is not possible experimentally to manipulate the hormonal state of humans. Nevertheless, some studies have been carried out on humans who, for various reasons, develop abnormal hormonal conditions. For example, a foetus can be exposed to unusual hormone levels if a mother receives hormone injections for medical reasons during pregnancy.

Several studies have indicated that females exposed to male hormones before birth often later exhibit more masculine gender-role behaviour than matched control groups of girls who were not exposed to the hormone (Money & Erhardt 1972; Hines, 1982). This suggests that hormones may control sex-related behaviour in humans as it does in animals. However, the interpretation of these findings is not so straightforward as might appear. Children exposed to abnormal hormones before birth are often born with some abnormality of the genitals. It is possible, therefore, that a girl's more masculine behaviour reflects her own, her parents' and possibly the investigator's reactions to her more masculine appearance. This research highlights the difficulty of separating out the effects of biological factors from socialisation processes.

Socialisation influences

Biological factors may pre-dispose males and females to adopt particular gender behaviour. However, most investigators agree that cultural influences and socialisation processes are the main determinants of an individual's gender role identity and behaviour. Debate continues, however, about how the child learns gender identity and roles, and when during development this learning occurs.

Three main theoretical approaches aim to explain the origins of gender role development: psychoanalytic theory; social learning theory, and cognitive-developmental theory.

Freud's Psychoanalytic Theory (see Chapter 4) suggests that during the phallic stage of development, the child encounters the Oedipus/Electra complex. Satisfactory resolution of this conflict results in the child identifying with the same sex parent. Thus the sex-appropriate attitudes and behaviour of the parent become internalised during the child's socialisation.

As has already been noted, psychoanalytic theory is open to much criticism and controversy, and verification of the existence of the Oedipus/Electra conplex has not been empirically established.

Social Learning Theorists maintain that sex role identity and behaviour are, like all behaviour, learned through the processes of **reinforcement** and **modelling**. Children are said to be shaped towards male or female roles. Boys and girls learn by being rewarded for sex-appropriate behaviour and punished for inappropriate behaviour, and by imitating the behaviour of male and female models such as their parents. Thus, boys may receive approval for aggressive behaviour, whereas girls would be penalised for the same behaviour; dependency may be encouraged in girls but frowned upon in boys.

Studies of socialisation influences

In studies of the development of sex role identity and behaviour, conclusions about whether boys and girls receive different socialisation experiences have varied. Below is a summary of some of the research evidence.

— Maccoby and Jacklin (1974) found little evidence that boys are reinforced for aggression and girls are reinforced for dependency. They concluded that infant and toddler girls and boys were treated very similarly. However, Maccoby and Jacklin may have failed to detect subtle differences in treatment.

— There is considerable evidence that people do respond differently to boys and girls on the basis of their expectations about what girls and boys are like. In a study by Rubin *et al.* (1974), parents were asked to describe their new-born babies as they would to a close friend. Even though boys and girls were very similar in health and in size and weight, they were described very differently. Boys were depicted as more alert, stronger and better co-ordinated than girls. Girls were described as smaller, softer and less attentive than boys.

— Smith and Lloyd (1978) have shown that boys are encouraged in more physical activities than are girls. Several other studies have shown that adults are more likely to offer a doll to a child they think is a girl and toys such as trucks or blocks to a child they think is a boy.

— There is growing evidence also that parents treat their young sons and daughters differently. Fathers are more likely to engage in physical rough and tumble play with their sons than with their daughters. Fagot (1978) showed that parents consistently show more approval when children behave appropriately to their sex and react negatively when girls or boys behave in an inappropriate way. Parents are likely to provide sex-appropriate toys for their children and encourage them to develop sex-typed interests (Maccoby & Jacklin, 1974).

— Studies show also that parents' expectations of achievement, particularly mathematical accomplishment, are lower for girls than for boys. Parents expect more independent performance from boys and are more likely to offer help to girls.

— Development of gender roles, like the acquisition of other complex behaviour, is unlikely to be the result solely of differential treatment and reinforcement. Therefore, many researchers have concerned themselves with how children may learn masculine or feminine behaviour by imitating same-sex models. Male and female stereotypes abound in literature and television as well as in the real world. How influential are these models during gender-role development? There is debate about how potent a force observational learning is in the development of gender roles. Huston (1983) claims that there is little firm evidence that children are more likely to imitate a model of the same sex than of the other sex. He suggests that the role of observational learning in the development of sex roles may be over-simplified. Characteristics of the model, such as power, competence and similarity, are likely to affect the modelling process. The child's perception of the situation and of the importance of gender are also important variables.

COGNITIVE-DEVELOPMENTAL THEORY

Kohlberg (1966) believes that the most important factor in the development of gender identity is the child's level of cognitive development. Early in life the child is labelled as boy or girl, and such categorisation leads to the child's perception of him or herself as masculine or feminine. This gender self-concept, coupled with the child's growing knowledge and understanding of gender, directs and organises his or her activities and ways of thinking. Thus a girl may, in effect, say 'I am a girl and I must behave like a girl'.

Kohlberg's theory cannot explain individual differences in gender role development, why, for example, some girls are highly feminine and others are more masculine. Processes such as identification and observational learning must also play a part.

CONCLUSIONS

1   It seems clear that no single process is responsible for the development of gender roles.

2   The influence of sex hormones and other biological factors probably predispose young children towards masculine or feminine characteristics.

3   At the same time, these naturally occurring differences are heightened by such factors as reinforcement from adults for sex-appropriate behaviour and the child's own perception of her/his gender.

4   The presence of sex-stereotyped models in books and on television, as well as those in the family, in the school and among peers, are likely also to play a part.

5   Individual differences in sex-role development probably arise from physiological and genetic factors, as well as the situations and people the child is exposed to.

SELF-ASSESSMENT QUESTIONS

1   What do you understand by 'sex-stereotypes'? Give an example of three characteristics usually associated with a female sex-stereotype.

2   Briefly describe the findings of Maccoby and Jacklin's study of sex differences. What problems arise in interpreting the findings?

3   Outline the biological explanation of gender role development. Evaluate a study which has been used to support the biological approach.

4   Briefly describe and evaluate one theoretical approach which suggests that gender roles are the product of social influences. Refer to at least one study which supports the approach.

5   Given the available evidence, what conclusions would you draw about the development of gender roles?

SECTION II: SELF AND SELF-ESTEEM

THE NATURE OF SELF

One of the most critical processes of the child's early years is the development of the sense of self. Psychologists have long been interested in what constitutes a well-developed sense of self. Gardner (1982) suggests that, initially, one must be aware of one's own body, its appearance, state and size. Secondly, one should be able to refer to oneself appropriately through language and be able to distinguish descriptions which apply to self and those which do not. Thirdly, one should be aware of one's own personal history: experiences one has had, skills and abilities acquired, one's needs and wishes. Such knowledge of self involves the ability to see oneself as others do, to develop a sense of self-awareness by taking account of the attitudes and perspectives of others. In addition to these ingredients, a mature sense of self includes a feeling of self-worth — an acceptance of and contentment with what one is like.

DEVELOPMENT OF SELF

In the early months of life, a child does not distinguish herself from the things around her. Gradually, however, the child develops an awareness of her/his own body as an entity separate from her/his environment. By the age of two, the child appears to have acquired some of the basic components of the sense of self, including the ability to use language appropriately to refer to him/herself.

Lewis and Brooks (1975) carried out a series of studies of the emergence of a sense of self in infants. Below is a summary of some of their findings.

Confronted with pictures of themselves, one year old babies generally call themselves 'baby'. Shortly before they reach two, most children start to use their own names and by two and a half can use personal pronouns. By the age of three, almost all children can refer to themselves in pictures using both their names and the correct personal pronouns.

In addition to using language correctly to refer to oneself, a sense of self involves the ability to recognise oneself as separate from other people. Lewis investigated infants' reactions to their own reflections in a mirror. A child's nose was secretly coloured with rouge and she was placed in front of the mirror. It was assumed that a child who recognised the reflection as herself might well touch her own nose.

The findings were that few nine to 12 month old children touched their noses, about two thirds of 21 month to two year old children did so. The older children also acted coy or touched the mirror image. These reactions suggest that an awareness of one's own person emerges during the second year of life.

Increasing self-awareness

Bannister and Agnew (1977) also illustrated children's increasing self-awareness with age. Groups of children of school age were asked a variety of questions about themselves and their home and school lives. The answers were tape-recorded and then re-recorded in different voices to disguise the identity of the original speakers. Four months later, the same children were asked to listen to the recordings and identify which statements were their own and which were not, and to give reasons for their choices.

Findings indicated that the children's ability to recognise their own statements increased with age. It was notable, also, that the children's explanations for their decisions reflected a growing knowledge of and confidence in their own feelings and beliefs. Thus, five year old children tended to rely on memory and simple clues contained in the statements, for example, 'That girl likes swimming and I swim, so I must have said that'. Nine year olds tended to use more complex methods for determining which statements were theirs and which were not. One child insisted that the statement 'I want to be a soldier when I grow up' was not his, because 'I don't think I could kill a human being so I wouldn't say I wanted to be a soldier'.

THE INFLUENCE OF SOCIAL FACTORS

Kuhn (1960) showed that as a child develops, the sense of self becomes less physically oriented and increasingly influenced by social factors. Groups of children and young adults were asked to respond to the questions 'Who am I?'. Only 25 per cent of statements made by seven year olds related to social roles such as 'I am a son', compared to 50 per cent of statements made by 24 year olds.

Writers such as Cooley (1902) Mead (1934), Argyle (1969) and Goffman (1971) have also highlighted the influence of interactions with other people on the development of self. The child's image of herself becomes the reflection of how she believes others see her.

ADOLESCENCE

Adolescence is a time of particular importance in the development of self

— (see Chapter 6). Erikson (1963) describes the 'identity crisis' which occurs during the teenage years. Faced with dramatic body changes and pressures arising from the need to make career and other important choices, the adolescent tries out different roles in order to 'find herself'. All the young person's cognitive and emotional capacities are brought to bear on the task of forming a coherent sense of who and what one is. Adolescence, too, sees an increase in the importance of the body image as an aspect of the sense of self.

SELF-ESTEEM

Self-esteem is that aspect of the self which is concerned with how we evaluate ourselves as people. It has been claimed that a major factor in the development of psychological illness is some individuals' feelings of inadequacy and unworthiness. The classic work of **Coopersmith** (1968) has shown marked variations in the behaviour of children who differ in self-esteem.

Coopersmith studied a group of children from the age of 10 until early adult life. Using a battery of tests and self-ratings, the sample was divided into three groups which were labelled 'high', 'medium' and 'low' self-esteem. High self-esteem boys showed themselves to be confident, active and academically and socially successful. Medium self-esteem boys had some of these qualities but were less confident of their worth and more in need of social acceptance. Low self-esteem boys were self-conscious, isolated, reluctant to participate in activities and constantly under-rated themselves. The boys all came from the same socio-economic background (middle class), and there were no significant differences between the groups in such things as intelligence and physical attractiveness.

A major difference between the groups arose from the characteristics and behaviour of the boys' parents. In general, **high self-esteem** boys tended to have parents who were also high in self-esteem. These parents, in contrast with the parents of low self-esteem boys, were more affectionate, and showed greater interest in and respect for their children as individuals. Methods of discipline were consistent and relied upon rewards for good behaviour and withdrawal of approval rather than physical punishment for bad behaviour.

Discipline in the homes of **low self-esteem** boys varied between highly punitive and over-permissive styles, and less clear guidance was given to the boys.

A follow-up of the sample into adult life has shown that the high self-esteem boys were more successful than low self-esteem boys, both educationally and in their careers.

Limitations of Coopersmith's study

One must be cautious when drawing conclusions from Coopersmith's study. Self-esteem is notoriously difficult to measure accurately. Asking children questions about how they evaluate themselves is a procedure which is open to biased responses: children may not want to admit that they have undesirable characteristics. Also, a limitation of Coopersmith's study is that he did not investigate the influence of socio-economic background or sex upon self-esteem; all the subjects were boys and from middle class backgrounds.

There is evidence to suggest that children from working class backgrounds typically exhibit lower self-esteem than those from homes higher up the socio-economic scale. In general, too, girls have lower self-esteem than boys. Even in primary schools where they often outshine boys, girls are inclined to under-rate their own abilities. Girls tend, also, to set themselves lower goals in life and to rate themselves lower on written measures of self-esteem than do boys. This is probably the result of cultural factors (see Section I of this chapter) and the general lower status of women in society (Fontana 1981).

Domain specificity

A more recent measure of self-esteem contains four sub-scales designed to measure three different aspects of a child's feelings of self-worth (Harter 1982) — cognitive, social and physical skills, together with general feelings of self-worth. Studies which have used this scale reveal that children often rate themselves differently in these different domains. Thus, their evaluation of their physical skills may differ from evaluation of their cognitive skills.

This is an important finding which should be understood by teachers and other people who work with children. Improving children's feelings of self-worth about their athletic competence does not necessarily make them feel good about their academic performance or improve their general feelings of self-worth.

SELF-ASSESSMENT QUESTIONS

1 What 'ingredients' are thought to make up the sense of self?

2 At what age is the sense of self thought to emerge? Briefly describe a study which supports your answer.

3 Outline a study which illustrates that development of the self is affected by social factors.

4 What do you understand by self-esteem? What are the problems encountered in measuring self-esteem?

5 What factors may influence the level of a child's self-esteem?

6 Why is it important for educators to be aware that self-esteem is domain-specific?

SECTION III: ACHIEVEMENT

How children think about themselves influences not only their interactions with others, but also their achievement and accomplishments in life. Two over-lapping lines of enquiry relating to achievement in children will be discussed: achievement-motivation and learned-helplessness.

ACHIEVEMENT-MOTIVATION

A child's achievement, both in school and in other aspects of life, depend not just on ability but on motivation. Those who strive to achieve are more likely to become high-fliers. Achievement-motivation is a construct proposed by psychologists to describe the tendency to set oneself high goals, to strive for success and to take pleasure in achievement.

In the 1940s Murray and his colleagues developed the Thematic Apperception Test (TAT), a projective test which measures an individual's motives, such as need for aggression and need for achievement. McClelland (1955) developed further the need for achievement (nAch) aspect of Murray's work. In studies of achievement-motivation, the subject is shown ambiguous pictures and asked to write stories to illustrate them. Analysis of the stories yields a score which reflects the subject's tendency to interpret the situation in the picture in terms of achievement and need for success. The TAT has been widely used as a measure of achievement-motivation, though it has been criticised by some psychologists as being too subjective.

Several studies have indicated that parents play an important role in the development of achievement-motivation. Parents who have high expectations of their child's ability to succeed and who offer firm but affectionate encouragement foster achievement-motivation in their children. Parents who are less warm and supportive and who are more domineering tend to have children who are low in achievement-motivation (Rosen & d'Andrade 1959).

School achievement

A child's level of achievement-motivation may vary in different subject areas and situations. A child may be very involved and keen to succeed in maths and science subjects, but make little effort in arts subjects. Another child may strive hard to succeed in athletics, but give up easily in maths. Studies have attempted to investigate some of the factors which determine a child's level of motivation in a particular subject area. Three of these factors are discussed below.

92

1   The **value** (attainment value) a child places on success in a particular subject area is thought to be one factor which affects her/his level of achievement-motivation. Parsons (1982) and her colleagues investigated achievement in maths in a large group of schoolchildren and adolescents. A battery of questions about motivations and attitudes was given to the students and their responses were later related to their grades in maths and to whether or not they chose to go on to advanced maths courses. Findings showed that the value the students attached to maths achievement was the best predictor of the students' later choice to take advanced maths.

2   Children's **expectancies of success** were found to be a factor in whether or not they were successful in maths. Parsons found that the best predictor of achievement in maths was the student's 'self-concept of ability' and expectancy of success in maths. Of course, one factor which determines the level of expectancy is whether one has experienced success or failure in the past. However, Parsons found that children who had performed similarly in the past often evaluated themselves differently and had different expectations about their future performance. For example, boys often had higher expectancy of future success than girls, even where their past performance was similar or lower.

3   Weiner (1974) proposes that **attributions** about success and failure are important determinants of achievement and expectations about future performance. Attributions are beliefs we form about the reasons for our own or someone else's behaviour. If people believe that their success or failure is caused by factors such as the degree of effort they themselves make, they are likely to strive to perform well. If, however, they attribute success or failure to factors such as luck or the difficulty of the task, they are likely to give up easily. Behaviour which arises from a belief that your successes do not arise from ability and that failures cannot be overcome by your own effort has been called 'learned helplessness' by some psychologists.

LEARNED HELPLESSNESS

Following on the work of Seligman and Maier (1967), who studied the concept of 'learned helplessness' in animals, Dweck *et al.* (1980) investigated this phenomenon in children. Dweck proposes that some children come to believe that the causes of their failures are outside their control. Consequently, when they do fail, they give up easily.

Dweck and colleagues carried out a series of studies in which they identified children who experienced learned helplessness. A question-naire was administered to the children asking for the reasons they succeed and fail in school.

Two groups of children were identified: one group of 'mastery oriented' children and a second group of 'learned-helpless' children. The mastery-oriented group attributed failures to their own lack of effort, while the learned-helpless children believed that failures arose from lack of ability or from external causes such as task difficulty or bad luck. The children were then given a series of problems to solve, some of which were solvable and some unsolvable. The mastery-oriented children viewed success as a reflection of their ability; where they failed, they increased their effort and looked for different strategies for solving the task. In contrast, the learned-helpless children viewed the reasons for failure as beyond their control and tended to relax their efforts to succeed.

Dweck believes that feelings of learned helplessness have particularly dire consequences in the area of mathematics. Unlike other subjects, mathematics continuously involves new concepts which may not relate to past learning, so providing many opportunities for early failures.

Dweck's findings led to a number of studies in which children were trained to attribute their failures to insufficient effort rather than lack of ability. After the training, many children's performance in maths improved. This method of training is much more effective than training which offers children continuous success. Apparently, helpless children are not simply children who are deprived of success, they are children who have difficulty in *correctly interpreting* their successes and failures. However, teaching children to attribute their successes to ability and their failures to insufficient effort may help to improve their achievements, but only where they possess the necessary skills and abilities. A child who increases her/his effort and still fails may have to conclude that failure results from lack of ability. This in turn may result in lowered self-esteem.

SELF-ASSESSMENT QUESTIONS

1 Explain the term 'achievement-motivation'.

2 What parental behaviour is thought to encourage the development of achievement-motivation in children?

3 Name and briefly explain three factors which may determine a child's level of achievement-motivation in a particular subject area. Outline one relevant study in this area.

4 What do you understand by 'learned helplessness' and how does it relate to achievement in children? Refer to a relevant study.

5 How might educators and other childcare professionals make use of the findings from research into achievement motivation and learned helplessness?

SECTION IV: CHILDREN'S FRIENDSHIPS

Children's conceptions of friendship have received attention from psychologists over the last decade or so. Methods of study tend to be based on Piaget's clinical interview method. Two main techniques have been used:

1   interviews which involve either questioning the child about who her/his best friend is and why, or asking the child to tell a story about friendship (Damon 1977);

2   stories are told to the child involving some kind of dilemma in relation to friendship; the child is then questioned about friendships and social relationships (Selman 1976).

Damon (1977) integrated the results of several studies which used different techniques and concluded that children's conceptions of friendship develop at three major levels:

At **level 1** (age approximately five to seven years) there is no real feeling of liking and disliking other children or any understanding of another person's internal thoughts or feelings. (This is in accord with Piaget's view that children of this age are egocentric). Friends are the playmates that children happen to mix with, usually in their home neighbourhood or at school. Friendships are easily started and ended and tend to centre on the sharing of material things such as toys and food.

At **level 2** (age eight to 11) children begin to appreciate the psychological aspects of friendship. Sharing mutual interests, trusting each other and responding to each other's needs are important aspects of friendship. Attributes such as kindness and consideration are critical in a friend.

At **level 3** (reached by about 12 years) friendship is seen as a deeper, more enduring relationship. The quality of friendship rests upon the extent to which the relationship involves mutual understanding and sharing of thoughts, feelings and secrets. Friends give psychological comfort and support to each other, especially in times of loneliness, sadness and fear.

While approximate ages have been given at each stage, it is important to note that children's level of friendship understanding is determined by the range of their experiences and the extent to which they reflect upon them, rather than their actual age.

OTHER ISSUES IN CHILDREN'S FRIENDSHIPS

Sex differences — Ahlgren and Johnson (1979) report that boys value competitiveness more than girls do, while girls stress co-operation. Up to adolescence, children tend to form friendships with others of the same sex. At adolescence, though children naturally become more interested in the opposite sex, differences between the sexes are still apparent. Unlike girls, boys appear to want to rebel against authority (Rubin 1980) while girls place a higher value on having an intimate confidant.

Clubs — During middle childhood, youngsters tend to form clubs or cliques — groups who have a mutual interest or who just wish to play together. Membership may centre upon popularity or skills possessed, but may also depend upon factors such as religion or race.

Similarity and friendship — In a longitudinal study of adolescent friendships Kandel (1978) investigated students' friendship choices, social attitudes and personality characteristics. The students were assessed both at the beginning and the end of the school year to compare similarities between friends in three friendship patterns:

1   maintained friendships (those friendships which existed both at the beginning and the end of the year);

2   dissolved friendships (friendships which existed at the beginning but not at the end of the year); and

3   newly-formed friendships (friendships which formed during the course of the year).

Kandel found that pairs of adolescents falling into patterns 1 and 3 were more like each other in attitudes and behaviour than were adolescent pairs falling into pattern 2. She concluded that:

(a)   similarity in behaviour and attitudes is important both in the selection of friends and in the maintenance of friendships;

(b)   friendships play a part in the socialisation of children: children who continued to be friends throughout the year resembled each other more at the end of the year than they did at the beginning, and new friends tended to adopt each other's characteristics.

SELF-ASSESSMENT QUESTIONS

1   What methods of study tend to be used in investigations of children's conceptions of friendship? Would it make sense to carry out experimental studies?

2   Briefly outline the developmental sequence in children's conceptions of friendship outlined by Damon.

3   What sex differences have been observed in children's friendships?

4   Describe a study which draws attention to the influence of friends on a child's socialisation.

FURTHER READING

Gardner H **Developmental psychology**. Little, Brown & Co., Boston, Toronto 1982.

Oakley A **Sex, gender & society**. Maurice Temple Smith 1972.

Rubin Z **Children's friendships**. Cambridge, Mass, Harvard University Press 1980.

"I BLAME MY PARENTS — THEY
NEVER SET ME ANY STANDARDS
WORTH REBELLING AGAINST."

Chapter 6

Adolescence and Adulthood

At the end of this chapter you should be able to:

1　identify and discuss physical and psychological changes that take place during adolescence;

2　assess alternative views of the factors which influence development during adolescence;

3　discuss studies of adolescence, particularly those which have considered the influence of the peer group;

4　consider theories and studies of development and change during early, middle and late adulthood;

5　discuss the impact of particular life events during adulthood, for example, marriage, parenting, divorce, unemployment, retirement, death and bereavement.

SECTION I: ADOLESCENCE

Sometime after the age of 10, humans mature sexually and become capable of reproducing. The period of time during which the reproductive processes mature is known as **puberty**. Although the most obvious signs of development during puberty are physical, changes also occur in cognitive functioning, social interactions, emotions and the sense of self. **Adolescence** is a longer period of time, and is generally defined as the period from the onset of puberty up to adulthood.

Adolescence has traditionally been considered a time of conflict and turmoil. G Stanley Hall, the first person to study adolescence scientifically, described it as a period of 'storm and stress' as well as of great physical, mental and emotional change. Currently, many clinical psychologists and psychoanalytic theorists still describe adolescence as a time of psychological disturbance though some recent studies of typical adolescents suggest that the extent of adolescent disturbance has been exaggerated (Conger 1977).

Physical changes during adolescence

During puberty, hormonal secretions from the pituitary gland, which lies at the base of the brain begin to stimulate the ovaries in females and testes in males, and the adrenal glands in both sexes. In males, reproduction depends upon the production of sperm cells, an event which usually occurs between 12 and 15 years. In females, the onset of the first menstrual flow, usually between the ages of 11 and 14, signals the production of ova. Certain changes which occur during puberty are known as **primary sexual changes**: ovulation in females is accompanied by an increase in the size of the vagina, clitoris and uterus, while in males enlargement of the penis and testes coincides with the production of sperm. In addition to these primary changes, a number of **secondary sexual changes** occur. These include, for both sexes, the development of pubic hair and changes in the shape and proportions of the body. In females, the breasts develop and in males the voice deepens and facial hair begins to appear. Both sexes experience the 'growth spurt', a substantial and rapid increase in height. The growth spurt in boys generally begins about two years later than it does in girls, and lasts for a longer period of time.

Late and early maturation

As noted above, the age at which young people reach puberty varies. Late or early maturation appears to have few psychological effects in girls. However, in males the picture is different. Boys who mature early are likely, because of their greater strength and size, to have an advantage in sports. They are also likely to develop earlier self-confidence in relationships with girls. The reverse is likely to be true for late-maturing boys. As a result, there are likely to be some personality differences between late and early maturing males. A large number of studies have indicated that late maturing males are likely to be more tense and self-conscious, less socially adept and to have greater feelings of inadequacy and rejection. In contrast, early maturers appear to be more self-assured and at ease with themselves. Follow-up studies indicate that these differences can persist into adult life. At age 33, most late maturers appeared to be less self-confident and controlled and more in need of support and help from others (Clausen 1975).

ADOLESCENT IDENTITY

According to Erikson (1968) adolescence is the stage of development during which the individual is searching for an identity. The crisis **'identity versus role confusion'**, encountered during adolescence is seen by many psychologists as the central crisis of all development. The major goal of the adolescent at this time is the formation of a secure and enduring **ego-identity**, or sense of self. Ego-identity has three important components:

1 a sense of unity, or agreement among one's perceptions of self;

2 a sense of continuity of self-perceptions over time; and

3   a sense of mutuality between one's perceptions of self and how one is perceived by others.

In order to arrive at a coherent sense of identity, adolescents typically 'try out' different roles without initially committing themselves to any one. Thus, stable attitudes and values, choices of occupation, partner and life-style gradually come together and make sense to oneself and others around.

Failure to achieve a firm, comfortable and enduring identity results in **role-diffusion**, or a sense of confusion over what and who one is. Over-strong pressure from parents and others may cause the young person to become bewildered and despairing, resulting in withdrawing, either physically or mentally, from normal surroundings. In the most extreme cases of role diffusion, adolescents may adopt a negative identity. Convinced that they cannot live up to the demands made by parents, the young people may rebel and behave in ways which are the most unacceptable to the people who care for them. So the son of a local Tory dignitary may join a left wing group, or the daughter of an atheist may become a devout member of a religious group.

Erikson's views arise mainly from clinical observations of both normal and troubled adolescents.

Parental styles

Parents play a significant part in determining how successful adolescents are in achieving an untroubled and enduring sense of identity. It has been shown that adolescents who are poorly adjusted and suffer a wide range of psychological problems are more likely to have experienced parental rejection or hostility than acceptance and love (Rutter 1980). In particular, the style of parental control is an important factor in the parent/child relationship. A number of studies have shown that **democratic, but authoritative**, parents are most likely to have children who, as adolescents, have high self-esteem and are independent and self-confident. Democratic/authoritative parents, while respecting the young person's right to make decisions, expect disciplined behaviour and give reasons for doing so (Elder 1980). Such rational explanations are important to adolescents who are approaching cognitive and social maturity and preparing to take responsibility for their own behaviour. In contrast, more **authoritarian** parents expect unquestioning obedience from their children and feel no need to explain reasons for their demands. Adolescents with authoritarian parents are likely to be less self-confident and independent, and more likely to regard their parents as un-affectionate and unreasonable in their expectations (Elder 1980; Conger & Peterson 1984).

TWO VIEWS OF ADOLESCENCE

The traditional view of adolescence is that of a period of development beset by turmoil and personal upheaval. Adolescence is characterised by extreme physical, emotional and cognitive changes, developing sexual urges, the need to make vocational and other choices, coping with pressure to conform to peer group expectations. All these factors exert pressure and contribute to the turmoil experienced by many young people.

The notion of adolescence as a time of storm and stress is taken for granted in many developmental theories, especially psychoanalytic theories. Anna Freud (1958), for example, describes the adolescent as experiencing renewed sexual feelings and strivings. The intensity of inner drives, she believes, leads to excessive emotional upset as the adolescent tries to cope with these impulses and desires.

The anthropologist, **Margaret Mead** (1939), challenged the traditional view of adolescence, questioning whether the western portrayal of adolescence as a troubled and tumultuous time was applicable in other cultures. Mead's study of life among preliterate peoples in the island of Samoa in the South Seas suggests that adolescent turmoil may result from cultural pressures that exist in industrialised, Western societies.

In Samoan life, boys and girls become familiar at an early age with the facts of life, death and sex. Sexuality is treated in an open, casual manner, and by adolescence, young people freely engage in sexual and love relations. The Samoan youth therefore experiences less guilt and shame than his/her Western counterpart, and is spared the anxiety and confusion often faced by Western adolescents.

Focusing on the course of adolescence in Samoan girls, Mead describes the process as smooth and natural — in sharp contrast with the adolescent years experienced in our society. Growing up in Samoa is easier because life in general is less complicated. Emotional relationships are treated casually, child rearing is treated lightly, competitiveness and ambition are almost non-existent. Consequently, adolescence is uneventful. In contrast, Western adolescents experience lives filled with opportunities, ambitions, pressures to achieve, and thus the stresses which accompany such lifestyles. Mead sees the wide range of opportunities and the pressure to make choices as fostering conflict and stress in adolescents of more 'civilised' societies.'

Mead did not conclude that we should try to remove the stresses that beset adolescents in our society. Rather, we should find ways of more adequately preparing young people for the range of personal and societal choices that they must face.

Mead's study has been criticised by some contemporary anthropologists. Freeman (1984), for example, claims that her account of life in Samoa was inaccurate and misleading. He attributed her 'errors' to a lack of understanding of the Samoan language and to her decision to live with American ex-patriots on the island rather than with the people she was studying.

Studies of adolescent turmoil

Masterson (1967) found evidence of anxiety in 65 per cent of a sample of normal adolescents aged between 12 and 18 years. Similar findings were reported by Rutter, Tizard and Whitmore (1970). Almost half of their sample of 14-15 year olds showed symptoms of emotional upset, such as depression or extreme misery.

In contrast, some studies failed to find evidence of stress or turmoil in adolescents. For example, Offer (1969) reported that for the majority of adolescents, changes in identity and in relations with parents and peers occurred gradually and without trauma. Dusek and Flaherty (1981) investigated the stability of self-concept in adolescents during a three-year longitudinal study. Responses to self-report questionnaires indicated that adolescent self-concept does not appear to undergo excessive change. The changes that were noted in subjects appeared to occur gradually and uneventfully.

The conclusions to be drawn from these inconsistent findings are that turmoil during adolescence is by no means inevitable. Some people adapt to the physical and psychological changes associated with adolescence with equanimity, while others experience feelings of self-doubt, resentment and anxiety.

ASPECTS OF ADOLESCENT EXPERIENCE

Cognitive growth

In his theory of cognitive development, Piaget (see Chapter 3) defined a new level of thinking which emerges around puberty - **formal operational thought**. Formal operational thought — the ability to reason and systematically test out propositions in the abstract without reference to concrete objects — is considered by Piaget to be the high point of human development.

According to Piaget, the adolescent, faced with a scientific problem to solve, is capable of reasoning hypothetically and taking account of a wide range of differing alternatives, as well as understanding the underlying scientific law. However, many studies have shown that true formal operational thought is found in our culture only among 30-40 per cent of adolescents and adults. Therefore, Piaget's claims do not seen strictly to apply to the majority of adolescents. It is nonetheless, clear that significant cognitive changes do occur during the adolescent years. Adolescent thought processes become more analytical and reflective than in younger children. They are more likely to use complex techniques as aids to memory, and are more likely to be capable of anticipating and developing strategies to deal with problems, both academically and in relation to social situations.

Kohlberg's work on **moral development** (see Chapter 4) has drawn attention to the way in which cognitive changes influence moral reasoning during adolescence. Moral values in the young child, at the pre-conventional level, are typically linked to external sources such as punishments and rewards. At the conventional level, in early adolescence, moral thought is dominated by concern for the family, society or national standards. Older and more experienced adolescents and adults, during the post-conventional or principled level, characteristically base moral judgements on the dictates of their own conscience.

Peer relationships

Peers play an important role in socialisation during adolescence. As young people become less influenced by family ties, they develop a greater affinity with others of the same age group. This trend is clearly illustrated in a study by Sorensen (1973). Sixty-eight per cent of his sample believed that their personal values were in accord with those of most other adolescents. Also, 58 per cent of the sample was more likely to identify themselves with others of the same age rather than with others of the same gender, community, race or religion.

A classic study by James Coleman (1961) drew attention to the so-called 'adolescent sub-culture' which exists in western societies. Such a subculture, Coleman believes, is substantially different from the adult culture and is responsible for orientating adolescents towards their peers and alienating them from their parents or the academic goals of their school.

More recent observers have been critical of the stereo-typed view of adolescent society portrayed by Coleman. McClelland (1982) suggests that, while many adolescent groups may distinguish themselves from adults through common tastes in clothing, hairstyles, music and so forth, not all these groups are necessarily in revolt against adult norms. According to Hartup (1983), adolescents are more likely to be influenced by parents than peers in such areas as moral and social values.

Peer relationships during adolescence tend to fall into three main categories.

1   **'Cliques'**, or small, intimate same-sex, and later both-sex, groups tend to be made up of young people of similar age, interests and social backgrounds. The clique is thought to provide the framework for the sorts of intimate personal relationships that formerly existed in the family setting.

2   Around the clique exists the **crowd**, the larger, more impersonal and loosely defined group. The crowd comes together mainly on the basis of similar social interests or future life-expectancies or career orientations. For instance, university bound or career minded 'A' level students might loosely constitute one crowd, while students who are training for skilled, manual jobs might constitute another.

3   As well as belonging to cliques and crowds, adolescents usually have one or two close friends. **Friendships** involve more intense and intimate relationships than do cliques and provide a setting for

young people to 'be themselves' and to express their innermost feelings, hopes and fears. Adolescents put a high premium on loyalty and trustworthiness in friends. Of almost equal value, especially for girls, is that a friend will listen and respond sympathetically to confidences. Berndt (1982) believes that adolescent friendships can enhance self-esteem by allowing individuals to feel that others respect and are interested in their ideas and feelings. Also, intimate friendships are likely to enhance later periods of development by contributing to the young person's social skills and sense of security.

Conformity

Popular stereotypes of adolescents suggest that they are a highly conforming group. Pressure from the peer group is said to motivate adolescents to conform to the customs, dress, values and so forth of the peer culture. Research suggests, however, that adolescents are no more likely to conform to peers than are younger children (Hartup 1983). Most studies indicate that conformity to peers peaks during middle and late childhood and declines during adolescence.

SELF-ASSESSMENT QUESTIONS

1   Briefly describe the physical changes which take place at puberty. Refer to some of the effects of late and early maturation.

2   Outline Erikson's views on the adolescent's search for an identity.

3   Contrast the traditional, Western view of adolescence with views of adolescence in a different culture.

4   To what extent does research support the inevitability of stress and turmoil during adolescence?

5   What cognitive changes occur during adolescence?

6   In what ways are peer relationships of importance during adolescence?

SECTION II:

LIFESPAN DEVELOPMENT: THE STUDY OF ADULTHOOD

Until relatively recently few developmental psychologists paid attention to the course of development during adulthood. Partly because two of the most important thinkers in the field, Piaget and Freud, did not consider the adult years, adolescence was treated as the last major period of development. More recently, however, research has been carried out into the nature and quality of adulthood, particularly old age. Investigations have viewed the adult years as a series of 'phases' linked both to age and to various milestones in life, or 'critical life events' such as marriage, parenting, divorce, unemployment, retirement, bereavement and death.

Few theories of adulthood have been proposed. However, a major theory which has embraced the entire lifespan from birth to old age is that of Erik Erikson (1963). Erikson has written extensively not only on childhood and adolescence, but on the developmental changes that take place during adulthood.

ERIKSON'S THEORY OF PSYCHOSOCIAL DEVELOPMENT

Erikson's (1963) theory attempts to provide a framework within which development throughout the whole lifespan may be viewed. A practising psychoanalyst, Erikson has been strongly influenced by the ideas of Sigmund Freud. However, whereas Freud described psycho**sexual** stages of development, Erikson emphasised the social forces which influence development. He describes a sequence of psycho**social** stages which he claims are applicable to individuals in different cultures and societies.

Erikson sees each stage of life as marked by a crisis, or struggle, which the individual must confront and attempt to resolve. The level of success with which the crisis is managed will determine that individual's psychological well-being at a particular time. The person who is unable to deal satisfactorily with a crisis will continue to experience problems in later stages and thus progress will be impaired. A brief account of Erikson's theory is set out in Figure 9. It includes an indication of the approximate ages covered by each stage of the lifespan.

Erikson's claim that the eight psychosocial stages of development are applicable universally to individuals in different societies is open to some doubt. The validity of the crises described at each stage and agreement about what constitutes a desirable outcome may depend heavily upon the norms and values of a particular culture. For example, stage 4, industry-v-inferiority, may only apply in cultures, such as ours, which place heavy emphasis on competitiveness and which frown upon children who do not succeed in particular skills at a given time.

A further examination of Erikson's views on adulthood will appear in the following sections on young, middle and late adulthood.

SELF-ASSESSMENT QUESTION

Briefly outline Erikson's theory of lifespan development. How far do you think his model can be applied to all human beings?

Figure 9

ERIKSON'S STAGES OF PSYCHOSOCIAL DEVELOPMENT

Life crisis	Favourable outcome	Unfavourable outcome
First Year		
Trust-v-mistrust The child needs consistent and stable care in order to develop feelings of security	Trust in the environment and hope for the future	Suspicion, insecurity, fear of the future
Second and third years		
Autonomy-v-shame and doubt The child seeks a sense of in-dependence from parents. Parental treatment should not be too rigid or harsh	A sense of autonomy and self-esteem	Feelings of shame and doubt about one's own capacity for self-control
Fourth and fifth years		
Initiative-v-guilt The child explores her enviroment and plans new activities. Sexual curiosity should be sympathetically handled by parents	The ability to initiate activities and enjoy following them through	Fear of punishment and guilt about one's own feelings
Six to 11 years		
Industry-v-inferiority The child acquires important knowledge and skills relating to her culture	A sense of competence and achievement. Confidence in one's own ability to make and do things	Unfavourable reactions from others may cause feelings of inadequacy and inferiority

Figure 9 (continued)

Life crisis	Favourable outcome	Unfavourable outcome
Adolescence (12-18 yrs)		
Identity-v-role confusion The young person searches for a coherent personal and vocational identity	Ability to see oneself as a consistent and integrated person with a strong, personal identity	Confusion over who and what one is
Young adulthood (20s and 30s)		
Intimacy-v-isolation The adult seeks deep and lasting personal relationships, particularly with a partner of the opposite sex	The ability to experience love and commitment to others	Isolation; superficial relationships with others
Middle adulthood (40-64)		
Generativity-v-stagnation The individual seeks to be productive and creative and to make a cõntribution to society as a whole	The ability to be concerned and caring about others in the wider sense	Lack of growth; boredom and over concern with oneself
Late adulthood (65+)		
Integrity-v-despair The individual reviews and evaluates what has been accomplished in life	A sense of satisfaction with one's life and its accomplishments; acceptance of death	Regret over omissions and missed opportunities; fear of death

SECTION III: YOUNG ADULTHOOD

GROWTH TRENDS

Following the sometimes turbulent and uncertain period of adolescence, the young adult is usually pre-occupied with self-growth in the context of society and relationships with others. According to Sheehy (1976) the central concern of 'Who am I?' during adolescence, shifts to questions such as 'How do I put my aspirations into effect?' or 'Where do I go from here?' during adulthood.

White (1975) identified five 'growth trends' observed during young adulthood.

1 **Stabilisation of ego-identity** — Ego-identity — one's feelings about oneself — is more firmly embedded than at any previous time during development. The ego cannot be seriously damaged, as it might have been during childhood or adolescence, by being called a failure, for example. Greater commitment to social roles, such as occupational role, and to other people, helps the individual to define and maintain a stable and consistent sense of self.

2 **Freeing of personal relationships** — Development of a stable view of themselves results in young adults becoming less concerned about themselves and able to develop strong personal relationships with others. This freedom allows them to be more responsive to another person's needs.

3 **Deepening of interests** — Young adults develop more commitment, and consequently achieve greater satisfaction, from interests such as hobbies, study, occupation, or personal relationships than do younger people.

4 **Humanising of values** — During this period young adults increasingly view moral and ethical problems in the light of life experiences. They are therefore more likely to be aware of the human aspects of values and the way these values apply in society.

5 **Expansion of caring** — A much more general concern for the well-being of others develops during early adulthood. This concern extends not only to particular individuals known personally to them, but in the wider sense to the deprived and suffering in society at large.

White emphasises that these growth trends represent the ideal goals of development during youth and young adulthood. Most people make some progress through the dimensions, though it is doubtful whether everyone fulfils all these goals.

LIFE EVENTS

Another way of considering adult development is to look at the way in which people adjust to important life events. A life event can be any 'happening' in the life of an individual which requires that individual to change the pattern of life. Some life events, such as marriage or starting a job, are experienced by most adults. Others, such as imprisonment or suffering a disabling accident, are experienced by relatively few people. Life-event theory suggests that all life events, whether good or bad, can induce stress and therefore require some psychological adjustment. (See 'Stressful life events' in the next section.)

Lowenthal, Thurhber and Chiriboga (1975) found that, as might be expected, young adults are in general exposed to more life events than are middle aged and older adults. The latter two groups report more negative stresses, while young adults report more positive stresses. Lowenthal *et al.* point out that the impact of a life event on an individual is not determined simply by the actual occurrence of the event. The critical factor in assessing the level of stress appears to be the individual's perception of the event. Two people might experience a similar life event, divorce, for example but perceive it in very different ways. One person might feel bereft, while another might feel liberated.

Marriage

There are many different kinds of marriage, each of which may sustain different roles for the husband and wife. Duberman (1973) has identified three main types of marriage.

1   The **traditional marriage** operates on the assumption that the husband is the main force and decision-maker. While the wife may have authority over such matters as child-care and domestic matters, all other areas are controlled by the husband.

2   In the **companionship marriage** the emphasis is on equality and companionship. Male and female roles are not differentiated and either partner may make decisions and assume responsibilities in any area.

3   The **colleague marriage** is similar to the companionship marriage in that heavy emphasis is placed upon sharing and personal satisfaction. However, role differences are accepted, and each partner becomes responsible for different areas of married life, according to their interests and abilities.

Companionship and colleague-type marriages are becoming increasingly common among middle-class couples. Many marriages, of course, do not fit neatly into any of these categories, and many features overlap.

Marital adjustment — Many studies have examined the changes and adjustments that people undergo when they marry. Vincent (1964) found that, in a group of married people, significant changes occurred in such traits as dominance and self-acceptance. Traditionally, greater adjustments to marriage have been made by women. Women often relinquish a career to become housewives and mothers and this may result in less contentment in marriage for women than for men. Bernard (1972) showed that married women have more psychological problems than married men or single women. Marriage appears however to have a beneficial effect on men. Married men report that they are happier than single men. They are also healthier and live longer (Veroff & Feld 1970).

Marital roles — Current social pressures regarding roles in marriage are less rigid than they were. Far more young people subscribe to the idea of shared roles in marriage, as compared to their parents' generation. As more women work outside the home, their husbands make greater contributions to household chores and childcare. Bahr (1973) reported that husbands of working wives perform significantly more household chores than husbands of non-working wives. However, Walker (1970) compared the work activity of husbands and wives in the home and showed that women spend far more time on household tasks than men (five hours a day compared to one and a half hours a day). A study by Booth (1977) showed that husbands of working women tended to be happier and under less stress than husbands whose wives were full time homemakers.

Divorce

Recent statistics indicate that approximately one in three marriages will end in divorce. Most of these divorces will occur during the first seven years of marriage (Reiss 1980). Teenage marriages are almost twice as likely to end in divorce as marriages that take place in the 20s.

The fact that marriages that break down tend to do so in the early years, and that teenage marriages are more likely to end in divorce, suggests that there may be some underlying developmental cause. One or the other of the marriage partners may not have firmly established a coherent identity independent of parents, or have succeeded in making a commitment to an occupation.

Adjustment to divorce — Studies suggest that divorce is highly stressful and ranks second only to the death of a spouse in terms of the re-adjustments which the individual must make in his or her life (Holmes and Rahe 1967). Emotional reactions to divorce will vary according to the events that preceded the break (Kelly 1982). For the unsuspecting, previously contented person, the reaction may be shock; the person who has suffered years of conflict and misery may well experience relief. However, evidence suggests that both will suffer distress and will experience a period of 'mourning' for the relationship.

Wiseman (1975) reports that many divorced people experience an identity-crisis as they reorganise their lives. This is particularly true for a woman who married young and whose identity was dominated by that of her husband.

Parenting

In Erikson's model of psychosocial development, the young adult experiences the crisis of **intimacy-v-isolation**. The need to feel love for and make a commitment to another person is the main goal of this stage. Following the resolution of this crisis, the first stirrings of the crisis of **generativity** occurs as couples confront feelings and make decisions about parenthood. Generativity — the desire to care for others and contribute to the growth and well-being of future generations - may be achieved through having children.

Fertility motivation — Many factors influence a couple's decision to have children. Researchers on fertility motivation — people's motives for having or not having children - have cited a number of factors which may contribute to the decision: social pressure, particularly from their own parents; a need for the emotional security that offsprings may give in later life; a desire to pass down one's own characteristics and values; a love of children for their own sake.

Parenthood as a developmental process — Many researchers believe that, for both parents, having a child contributes to the developmental process in that it allows them to relive the earlier developmental crises through which they themselves have passed. Erikson (1968) believes that pregnancy allows a woman to use the 'productive inner space' which lies at the centre of female fulfilment. Benedek (1959), a psychoanalyst, suggests that a woman's maternal instinct arises from her early identification with her own mother. Memory traces retained from her own childhood allow her to re-experience the pleasures and problems of infancy as she looks after her own child. Dinnerstein (1976), however, believes that a woman's feelings about mothering would be different if child-care were shared more evenly with the father.

Adjusting to parenthood — A major task of parenthood is to socialise the infant. The parents, in turn, are socialised by the child. As the parents help the child to acquire good eating, toilet and social habits, they learn how to respond to the child and make it comfortable and secure.

Parenthood has been described as a crisis point in the life of a couple. In a study of over 2,500 adults, Dohrenwend *et al.* (1978) found that the birth of the first child was rated the sixth most stressful life event in a list of 102 possible events. This may be at least in part because people receive little preparation for parenthood from society.

Many studies have indicated that marital satisfaction tends to decrease with the arrival of the first child (Belsky *et al.* 1983). Schulz (1972) found that young parents talk to each other only about half as much as couples without children, and then the conversation is often about the child. In some marriages, however, particularly if children are planned, they can strengthen the marital relationship.

Parenthood invariably leads to the couple relating to society in a new way. New mothers enjoy the company of other new mothers; young parents seek out the company of their own parents for advice and emotional support — and for babysitting. Social institutions which previously have had little significance in the lives of the couple will be re-evaluated. Parks, libraries and schools will be assessed, and active involvement may occur in causes such as the promotion of road safety or opposition to TV violence (Brodzinsky *et al.* 1986).

SELF-ASSESSMENT QUESTIONS

1 Describe White's account of development during young adulthood.

2 What do you understand by the term 'life events' as used in psychological literature?

3 Discuss some of the research carried out into the impact of either marriage or divorce.

4 What psychological adjustments must be made during parenthood? To what extent are parents socialised by the child?

SECTION IV: MIDDLE ADULTHOOD

There are two conflicting interpretations of the nature of middle age. One view is that it is a time of conflict and crisis. Researchers have used the term 'mid-life crisis' to describe the time when middle-aged people become conscious of, and often depressed about, the changes which are taking place in their lives, such as the physical and psychological effects of ageing, occupational adjustments and the departure of children from the home. A more optimistic view emphasises that middle age is a time when people are more accepting of themselves and are ready to approach life with renewed vigour.

Which of these two interpretations is adopted by middle-aged people depends upon how they perceive themselves and their lives. So, too, does the timing of the advent of middle age. Some people perceive themselves to be young or middle-aged well into their 60s, whereas others consider themselves middle-aged at 35.

PERSONALITY AND SOCIAL DEVELOPMENT

A leading question that has been addressed by researchers is 'Do aspects of personality, such as values and beliefs, change systematically as people move from young adulthood to middle and old age, or is personality stable throughout life?'. Unfortunately, the answer to this question is not easy to obtain. Personality is a very complex aspect of human beings, and not easy to measure accurately over time. However, in general, empirical evidence supports the notion of stability of personality in adulthood.

Longitudinal studies, in particular, note that some of the most stable characteristics include values (social, political, economic, religious and aesthetic) and vocational interests. Neugarten (1977) reports that in cross-sectional studies the findings are less clear-cut, with some studies, though not others, finding differences between age groups in personality characteristics such as rigidity, cautiousness, conservatism and self-concept. (See Chapter 1 for an indication of the strengths and limitations of longitudinal and cross-sectional studies.)

Studies of personality over time have distinguished between **relative stability** and **absolute stability**. Relative stability refers to the rank order of personality scores of a sample of subjects over a period of time. A personality dimension would be relatively stable if the rank order among subjects remained similar from one period to another, irrespective of whether there was an over-all increase or decrease in the scores. Absolute stability refers to whether subjects maintain the same score on a personality dimension from one occasion to another. For example, it is known that people increase their level of self-awareness between childhood and middle age. The absolute stability of this personality dimension is therefore low.

Haan and colleagues (1981) carried out a major longitudinal study of personality and physical and mental health in several cohort groups from adolescence to middle age. Subjects' personality ratings were correlated across the adolescent, young adult and middle adult years. Results showed the following.

1 Generally, personality dimensions were relatively stable, that is, subjects rated high on particular dimensions on one occasion tended to be rated high on a later occasion.

2 Greater stability existed between adolescence and young adulthood, and between young adulthood and middle adulthood, than between adolescence and middle adulthood.

3 Those personality dimensions most concerned with the self, for example self-confidence, tended to be the most stable.

4 Women's personalities tended to be more stable than men's.

5 Men's personalities changed most during the period from adolescence to young adulthood, as they developed careers and financial independence.

6 People increased in cognitive investment, openness to self, nuturance towards others and self-confidence from adolescence to old age; that is, there is a low degree of absolute stability in these dimensions.

Conclusions

People change slowly and moderately between adolescence and middle age, that is, there is a low degree of absolute stability. However, since significant, if only moderately high, correlations were found over time for some personality characteristics, a moderate degree of relative stability in personality is maintained. It can therefore be concluded that while some developmental change does occur, adult personality development is not subject to large and pervasive changes in beliefs, attitudes and values.

DEVELOPMENTAL THEORIES OF MIDDLE ADULTHOOD

Erikson (1963) considers the central conflict of the middle years to be that of **generativity versus stagnation**. The individual becomes concerned with contributing to and guiding the next generation. Erikson explains that this drive does not necessarily relate to one's own children, but may take the form of creative contributions or guidance and counselling with young people. The person who does not achieve generativity will experience a sense of personal impoverishment and an excessive concern with self.

Peck (1968) described four major psychological adjustments which face middle aged people.

1   They must learn to value wisdom more than physical power and attractiveness. This involves accepting as inevitable the decline in physical powers and gaining satisfaction from the wisdom that comes from experience, knowledge and mental ability.

2   Men and women must value each other as individual personalities rather than as primarily sex objects.

3   They must develop the capacity to shift their emotional investment from one person or activity to another. Emotional flexibility is particularly important in middle age. As children leave home, relatives or friends die and certain activities such as strenuous sport are no longer possible, it is important to be able to focus on and gain satisfaction from different people or activities.

4   It is important at middle age to remain mentally flexible and receptive to new ideas and ways of doing things.

Levinson *et al.* (1977) view the years of middle adulthood as a time for the consolidation of interests, goals and commitments. Somewhere between the early 30s and about 40, people begin to 'settle down'. Stable commitments are made to family, career, friends, or some special interest.

The transition to middle life occurs around 40 and lasts for about five years. This transitional period forms a link between early and middle adulthood, and is a time when people evaluate themselves. This re-evaluation involves measuring their achievements in the light of earlier goals and, where necessary, re-adjusting these goals. Levinson believes that the individual must come to terms with discrepancies between what was aimed for earlier in life, and what the reality is now. If this acceptance is achieved the individual will experience stability during middle adulthood.

Levinson notes that qualities such as wisdom and compassion often emerge during middle adulthood.

These three theorists each describe a different facet of middle age. A common theme exists in that each agrees that middle adulthood is a period of significant challenge, during which individuals must adjust to changes both within and outside of themselves.

STRESSFUL LIFE EVENTS

A factor in the lives of middle aged adults which is currently receiving attention from researchers is the question of stress and its effects on health and psychological well-being. A study by Theorell and Rahe (1974) indicated a positive relationship between the incidence of heart attacks and the number and type of stressful life events such as death of a spouse, loss of job, or divorce. (See 'Life events' in section on Young Adulthood.)

Measuring life stress

Psychologists have developed ways of measuring the level of stress associated with particular life events, as well as the over-all level of stress experienced by the individual. Figure 10 shows one such measure, the Social Re-adjustment Rating Scale (SRRS), which was developed by Holmes and Rahe (1967). Subsequent studies which have employed this measure report that the higher the level of stress experienced by individuals, the greater the incidence of health problems.

Rating scales such as SRRS have been criticised as being too primitive and crude a measure of the impact of stressful life events. For example, Brown *et al.* (1973) points out that people vary in their responses to stressful events. What is traumatic for one person may actually be beneficial to another. Brown suggests also that individuals should be interviewed to work out their level of 'contextual threat', a measure of the circumstances surrounding a stressful life event.

Unemployment during middle age

Unemployment is an extremely stressful occurrence for adolescents and adults of all ages. However, the unemployment rates caused by recession are likely to have more serious outcomes for older adults. Middle-aged and older adults, once unemployed are likely to remain so for up to 70 per cent longer than younger workers (Entine 1976). The psychological

Figure10

SOCIAL RE-ADJUSTMENT RATING SCALE
(From Holmes and Rahe, 1967)

Rank	Life Event	Mean Value
1	Death of spouse	100
2	Divorce	73
3	Marital separation	65
4	Jail term	63
5	Death of close family member	63
6	Personal injury or illness	53
7	Marriage	50*
8	Dismissal from work	47
9	Marital reconciliation	45
10	Retirement	45
11	Change in health of family member	44
12	Pregnancy	40
13	Sex difficulties	39
14	Gain of new family member	39
15	Business re-adjustment	39
16	Change in financial state	38
17	Death of a close friend	37
18	Change to different line of work	36
19	Change in number of arguments with spouse	35
20	Mortgage over £10,000	31
21	Foreclosure of mortgage or loan	30
22	Change in responsibilities at work	29
23	Son or daughter leaving home	29
24	Trouble with in-laws	29
25	Outstanding personal achievement	28
26	Wife begins or stops work	26
27	Begin or end school	26
28	Change in living conditions	25
29	Revision of personal habits	24
30	Trouble with boss	23
31	Change in work hours or conditions	20
32	Change in residence	20
33	Change in schools	20
34	Change in recreation	19
35	Change in church activities	19

Figure 10 (continued)

Rank	Life Event	Mean Value
36	Change in social activities	18
37	Mortgage or loan less than £10,000	17
38	Change in sleeping habits	16
39	Change in number of family gatherings	15
40	Change in eating habits	15
41	Holiday	13
42	Christmas	12
43	Minor violations to the law	11

* Marriage was arbitrarily assigned a stress value of 50. No event was found to be any more than twice as stressful. Here the values are reduced proportionally and range up to 100.

An individual's level of stress is calculated in the following way.

1. The subject is asked to describe specific life events experienced during a particular period of time, for example the past two years.

2. The appropriate stress value for each life event is assigned to the person and a total stress index is arrived at by adding together all the stress values the person has received.

consequences for middle-aged adults are also likely to be serious. Family responsibilities will probably be very demanding and the need to save and build up financial security for old age is likely to be at its most pressing.

A study by Powell and Driscoll indicates that unemployed adults progress through four psychological stages during a prolonged period of unemployment.

1   **Relaxation and relief** occurs after the initial shock. Individuals experience a feeling of contentment with their new, more relaxed status. Feelings of hope and confidence in their ability to find new employment lead to phase 2.

2   A **concerted effort** is made to secure a new job. At this stage, most are becoming bored with their increased leisure time, but are still

optimistic about job prospects. As efforts to find work are continually frustrated, the jobless person enters a third phase.

3 **Vacillation and doubt** — The individual begins to experience self-doubt and efforts to find work are irregular. Relations with family and friends become strained.

4 **Malaise and cynicism** — The last phase is characterised by feelings of apathy and listlessness. Many of the people studied claimed that they felt helpless and inadequate and had difficulty in imagining themselves ever working again.

SELF-ASSESSMENT QUESTIONS

1 What do you understand by the term 'mid-life crisis'?

2 What conclusions would you draw from research carried out to investigate the stability of personality over time? Distinguish between absolute stability and relative stability.

3 Discuss one developmental theory of middle adulthood.

4 For what purpose is the Social Re-adjustment Rating Scale used? In what way has this scale been criticised?

5 Briefly discuss a study which has examined the psychological impact of unemployment.

SECTION V: LATE ADULTHOOD

Old age is the last phase of the lifespan. Gerontologists (gerontology is the name for the scientific study of the elderly) have attempted to define when exactly the period of old age begins. Some distinguish between 'elderly' and 'advanced' old age. Early old age is said to occur between the ages of 65 and 74, and late old age from 75 on. However, a chronological definition of ageing can be misleading. The adage 'You are as old as you feel' is subscribed to by many older adults. This implies that subjective or psychological factors are more important in defining whether or not a person is old, than is noting the number of years lived.

The study of older adults has gathered momentum over the last 20 years or so. As life expectancy increases, older people have become the focus of attention by psychologists, medical practitioners, urban planners and politicians. Among gerontologists, many disagreements arise about late adulthood. Some find that intellectual ability declines with age; others refuse to accept that this is so. Some believe that successful adjustment to old age is brought about by the individual's disengagement from society; others believe that continued activity actually enhances adjustment in later years.

SENESCENCE

Senescence, or primary ageing, refers to the period of life when the degenerative processes of ageing set in. It is a normal part of growing older and usually occurs gradually. The timing and effects of senescence vary from person to person.

Researchers have identified many different aspects of senescence. These include physiological, biochemical and behavioural changes. As people age there is a loss of neural tissue; the heart, lungs and nervous system become less efficient; and the body's resistance to disease breaks down. Older people are thus more likely to become ill and have greater difficulty in recovering. Many of the external signs of senescence begin to appear during middle age: grey hairs, skin wrinkles, weight gain, diminishing muscle strength and agility, sight and hearing difficulties are all outward manifestations of the changes which occur with increasing age.

COGNITIVE FUNCTIONING

Certain aspects of intelligence appear to decline with age.

IQ — Longitudinal studies indicate that performance on IQ tests is relatively stable up to the age of around 60. After this, a steady decline is often noticeable in areas which measure psycho-motor skills, attention, memory, inductive reasoning and quickness of response. However, social knowledge, verbal-conceptual ability and mathematical reasoning do not appear to be affected by the ageing process (Horn & Donaldson 1980).

Decreases in intellectual functioning do not seem to be experienced equally by all people. A study by Schulz, Kaye and Hoyer (1980) found that those who had kept themselves mentally active throughout their lives, experienced little, if any, decline.

Memory — Studies of memory processes during old age indicate that short-term memory, that is the recall of immediate information that is still being attended to, suffers some decline. There appears to be little difference between older and younger adults in the number of items that can be held in short-term memory. The older adult, however, is likely to be more susceptible to distraction and less able to recall memorised information in a different form.

So far as long-term memory is concerned, research indicates that older people have more problems remembering material that they have ceased actively to focus upon, though they will have little difficulty remembering knowledge and experiences that they recall frequently.

As with general intellectual functioning, well-educated and mentally active individuals do not experience the same memory decline as those people who do not exercise their minds.

Many researchers stress that although some aspects of cognitive functioning do show decline, this should not lead to an overly pessimistic view of old age. As people age, deficits in physical and mental functioning are often compensated for by greater wisdom arising from experience and breadth of knowledge.

The cognitive quality of **wisdom** incorporates such characteristics as intuitiveness, experience, introspection, empathy, understanding, patience and gentleness. Clayton and Birren (1980) note that most adults associate these characteristics with old age.

THEORIES OF PERSONALITY DEVELOPMENT AND ADJUSTMENT

Late adulthood is seen by many theorists as a time of continuing psychological growth. The developmental tasks of the older adult include adjusting to declining physical powers and health, coping with retirement and limited income, and adjusting to the death of a marriage partner.

Erikson's theory

During old age, according to Erikson (1968), the individual must resolve the crisis he describes as **ego-integrity-v-despair**. As people approach the end of their lives they tend to look back and evaluate the decisions they have made and the actions which have influenced their lives. This review should ideally lead to feelings of satisfaction and acceptance that the life one has lived is meaningful and important. Such feelings lead to high ego-integrity. The person whose life review reveals feelings of regret and disappointment that life has been unsatisfactory and unfulfilling will experience despair.

While most people will experience both these psychological states at various times, the person who achieves a greater degree of integrity over despair will experience a feeling of well being and a sense of purpose even in the face of death.

Peck's theory

Peck (1968) believes that continued psychological growth during late adulthood depends upon how well individuals cope with three major developmental tasks.

1   They must come to terms with **vocational retirement**. This involves developing feelings of self-worth and satisfaction in areas other than the job of work which has been a central influence in earlier stages of life. People able to express their personalities in ways not connected with their work-role are more likely to lead happy, interesting and well adjusted lives in later years.

2   **Physical decline** is inevitable in old age. People who have relied upon physical well-being for satisfaction and pleasure may become

very pre-occupied with the state of their bodies and depressed about their declining physical powers. Peck believes that it is important that older people should shift their attention away from bodily concerns and learn to value satisfying relationships with others and creative mental activities.

3 The final adjustment that older adults must make is related to **human mortality**. Each individual must recognise and accept that death is inevitable. Such acceptance should include the knowledge that their lives can be significant after death through children, through friendships and through contributions they have made to society.

SUCCESSFUL ADJUSTMENT TO AGEING

What constitutes successful adjustment to old age has been the subject of some debate. There are two prevalent, largely conflicting theories: disengagement theory and activity theory:

Disengagement theory proposes that as individuals approach their last years of life, they gradually withdraw from social contacts and activities. They also become less concerned with the problems of the outside world and detach themselves from complicated emotional interactions with other people.

Studies (Neugarten 1973, 1977) suggest that older people increasingly take less part in family and community activities. This does not mean that friends and social relationships are not important to them. In fact, friendships can often provide valuable support and compensate for losses experienced in old age. Therefore, friendship and social interaction can help the adjustment process during ageing (Tesch 1983).

Disengagement theory was first proposed by Cumming and Henry (1961) who maintain that the gradual disengagement of the individual from society will lead to psychological well-being and contentment. However, premature disengagement caused by ill health or early retirement is likely to lead to problems in adjustment.

Activity theory suggests that successful adjustment during old age is brought about by the individual remaining productive and active. Psychological well-being is maintained where an individual can find substitute activities for those that are ending. For example, retirement from work will require the individual to find new interests and activities to fill the gap.

Activity theory has received little empirical support and has been criticised as an over-simplification of the issues involved. Some individuals clearly prefer to maintain a high level of involvement in social activities and relationships, while others are more contented with disengagement.

Also, factors other than personality or the ageing process may partially determine whether an individual disengages from society or continues to lead an active life. Lack of money, reduced mobility, societal attitudes towards old people may all militate against an individual leading an active, independent life in old age.

Studies by Reichard, Livson and Peterson (1962) indicate that personality factors are important determinants of whether a person will adjust successfully to old age. Therefore, neither disengagement nor activity theories alone can adequately explain successful ageing.

RETIREMENT

Most people retire from full time work during their 60s. The exact age at which people retire is usually determined by our social security system which decrees that 60 for a woman and 65 for a man are the appropriate ages. While some people approach retirement with pleasurable anticipation and relief, others consider themselves not yet ready to relinquish what is often a meaningful and important part of their lives.

Psychological impact

Because of the emphasis placed on the importance of work in our culture, retirement presents most people with a substantial sense of loss. Loss of identity, social role, financial security and prestige require that significant psychological adjustments are made. However, research has indicated that, contrary to popular belief, retirement is not associated with decline in health and psychological well-being. For example, Streib and Schneider (1971) observed that, except for people who are compulsorily retired, it does not appear to lead to low morale. Troll (1982) notes that, for many people, health improves in the early post-retirement years.

The retirement process

Retirement is often thought of as a life event which happens suddenly, usually in late adulthood. However, some researchers view retirement as a developmental process which takes place gradually over a period of time.

Atchley (1977) suggests that the process of retirement involves seven phases, (see Figure 11) though not all people necessarily pass through every stage.

Phase 1 — The **remote phase** usually occurs during middle adulthood. At this time most working adults are fully immersed in their jobs and may have only vague thoughts about retirement. Little or no preparation for retirement is made at this time.

Phase 2 — As the time for retirement approaches, people enter the **near pre-retirement phase**. At this time much active thought and planning

Figure 11

ATCHLEY'S 'PHASES OF RETIREMENT'

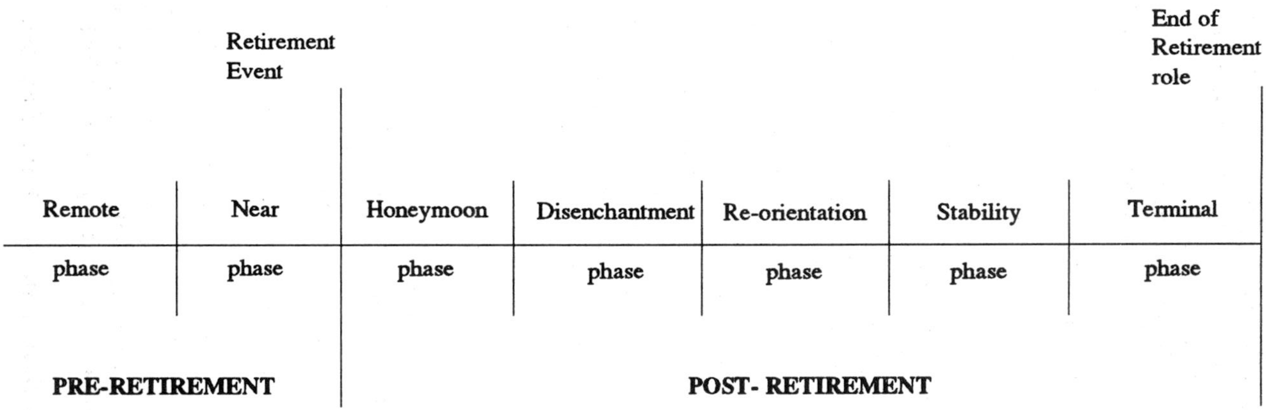

Remote	Near	Honeymoon	Disenchantment	Re-orientation	Stability	Terminal
phase	phase	phase	phase	phase	phase	phase

Retirement Event

End of Retirement role

PRE-RETIREMENT

POST - RETIREMENT

124

for retirement occur. The individual gradually disengages from some of the duties and responsibilities of the job.

Phase 3 — The actual retirement is often accompanied by feelings of pleasure and anticipation — the **honeymoon phase**. Many of the activities previously planned can now be engaged in.

Phase 4 — Retirement activities often prove to be less satisfying than expected. When this happens the individual enters the **disenchantment phase** and feels depressed and 'let down'.

Phase 5 — Disenchantment is usually followed by a **re-orientation phase** during which people face up to the reality of retirement. The individual contemplates the future and attempts to develop a realistic view of its alternatives.

Phase 6 — There next follows what Atchley terms the **stability phase** when people settle to the routines of retirement with realistic awareness of their own capabilities and limitations. In the stability phase, people can be said to have fully adjusted to the role of the retired person.

Phase 7 — The **terminal phase** occurs when for one reason or another the retirement role ends. This may happen because individuals become ill or disabled and can no longer care for themselves. For some people the role of retiree is terminated when they seek out employment once again.

Atchley's phases of retirement may not apply in the same form and sequence to everyone. Individual differences in personality, variations in the age at which people retire and the reasons why they retire will all influence the process of retirement. However, his model aids our understanding of the developmental tasks which are faced by most older people who are making the transition from the role of worker to that of non-worker.

DEATH AND BEREAVEMENT

In Western cultures the subject of death is a sensitive issue which, in the past, has been frequently avoided. Metaphors such as 'passed away' or 'no longer with us' have been used to describe the occurrence of death. Over the past two decades there has been a considerable shift in attitudes towards dying. Doctors and psychologists have attempted to view death, not as a distinct event which terminates life, but as an important **process** in the life cycle.

Previously, doctors and family members have tended to withhold the truth from a dying person, on the basis that it was kinder to do so. Today, however, most doctors recognise that a dying person needs to be aware of her/his condition in order that the necessary psychological adjustments and practical arrangements may be made (Schulz 1978).

Kuhler-Ross's Stages in the Dying Process

Kuhler-Ross (1969) studied over 200 terminally ill people. On the basis of her observations and interviews with the patients, she proposed that the dying process consists of five stages through which the dying person passes as death approaches.

1   **Denial** — Most people, on learning that they are terminally ill, react with shock followed by a sense of disbelief. They may assert that there has been an error in diagnosis and that the doctors are incompetent. Denial can be observed in almost all patients and is considered to be a fairly healthy way of coping with the initial shock.

2   **Anger** — As denial becomes difficult to sustain, the dying person typically experiences anger at her/his condition and resentment of the healthy. 'Why me?' is a common cry. Kuhler-Ross believes that it is important for the person's caretaker to understand why and how the anger originates, and to empathise with the patient.

3   **Bargaining** — At this stage the person adopts a different approach and attempts to bargain with God for an extension of life or a period of time without pain and discomfort. A patient may promise, for example, a life dedicated to the church, or donation of organs to medical research in return for a postponement of death.

4   **Depression** — When terminally ill patients can no longer deny their illness and when more severe physical symptoms occur or hospitalisation is necessary, a sense of deep loss is experienced. Kuhler-Ross distinguishes between two kinds of depression which occur at this time.
    Reactive depression results from the loss already suffered, for example, loss of physical strength or job. Preparatory depression relates to the loss that is to come, for example, loss of loved ones and treasured possessions. Kuhler-Ross believes that encouragement and reassurance are helpful to people suffering reactive depression. However, patients suffering preparatory depression must be allowed to express emotions and prepare for impending loss.

5   **Acceptance** — In this final stage, the dying person accepts death. If they have been allowed time to work through the earlier stages and have been given some assistance to do so, they will feel no anger or depression. Quietness and gentle companionship are appreciated and they appear emotionless and detached.

Not all terminally ill people move through the stages described by Kuhler-Ross. For example, a person may die in the anger stage because he or she is psychologically incapable of moving beyond it, or because the rapid progression of the illness does not allow the time to do so.

Care of the dying

One important outcome of Kuhler-Ross's study of dying people is the realisation by doctors and other medical workers that dying persons need sensitive care as they prepare for death. Many terminally ill patients face death alone in a sterile and impersonal hospital ward without the support and companionship of family and friends.

A more humane approach towards the care of the dying is slowly gaining ground with the emergence of the **hospice** movement. A hospice is an establishment which provides a homelike and emotionally supportive setting for terminally ill people. The emphasis is on keeping the patient comfortable and free from pain and providing companionship as the patient prepares for death. Family and friends are encouraged to help with the care of the patient. The hospice movement arose from the work of the British doctor, Cicely Saunders.

Bereavement

Bereavement is the condition or state of loss and is most often experienced when someone close to us dies. However, bereavement may result from other losses such as loss of a close relationship through divorce or the loss of a job because of redundancy.

Grief is a person's emotional response to bereavement. The grieving process involves psychological suffering. However, it has been suggested it is a necessary process and people who do not grieve are unlikely to recover from their loss.

Clayton *et al.* (1971) identified the 'symptoms' most commonly associated with the grieving process. In a study of 109 recently bereaved widows, the most common symptoms reported by more than 80 per cent of the respondents included crying, depression and insomnia. Over half suffered from loss of appetite and had difficulty concentrating.

Recent research indicates that bereavement can produce changes in nervous, hormonal and respiratory systems and can weaken the immune system (National Academy of Sciences 1984). Bereaved persons are therefore at risk of suffering physical or mental illness.

Stages of bereavement

Bowlby (1980) identified five stages in the grieving process:

1 concentration on the deceased person;

2 anger towards the deceased or other people;

3 appeals to others for help;

4 despair, withdrawal, disorganisation;

5 reorganisation and focus on a new object of interest;

Kavanagh (1974) suggests seven stages of bereavement.

1 shock,

2 disorganisation,

3   violent emotions,

4   guilt,

5   loneliness and loss,

6   relief,

7   re-establishment.

Recovering from grief is greatly aided if the bereaved person is able to express emotions and concerns about the death to a sensitive listener.

Bereavement in general lasts between one and two years. If satisfactory adjustment is made during the grieving process, the person is able to establish new interests and relationships. Memories of the dead person are likely to be pleasant rather than painfully associated with the experience of the death.

SELF-ASSESSMENT QUESTIONS

1   Briefly describe some of the physical changes which occur during senescence.

2   To what extent does cognitive functioning decline with age?

3   Outline one theory of personality development during late adulthood.

4   Contrast two theories concerned with successful adjustment to old age.

5   Outline Atchely's seven 'phases of retirement.' What factors may cause variations in the way people react to the process of retirement?

6   In what ways can the findings of psychological research be of help to those who care for the dying?

7   Discuss some of the physical and psychological effects of bereavement.

FURTHER READING

Brodzinksky D, A Gormley and S Ambron **Lifespan human development**. HRW International Editions 1986.

Coleman J C **The nature of adolescence**. Methuen 1978.

Conger J J **Adolescence & youth**. Harper & Row 1984.

Dohrenwend B S & B P Dohrenwend **Stressful life events: their nature & effects**. Wiley 1974.

Turner J S & D Helms **Lifespan development**. Saunders London 1979.

References

Ahlgren A & D W Johnson (1979) Sex differences in co-operative and competitive attitudes from the second through the twelfth grades. **Developmental Psychology** 15, 45-9.

Ainsworth M D S (1967) **Infancy in Uganda**. Baltimore, John Hopkins University Press.

Ainsworth M D & B A Wittig (1969) Attachment and exploratory behaviour in 'a strange situation'
in: B M Foss ed. **Determinants of infant behaviour** Vol 4. Methuen.

Ainsworth M D, S M Bell & D J Stayton (1974) Infant/mother attachment and social development as a product of reciprocal responsiveness to signals in: M P M Richards ed. **The integration of the child into a social world**. Cambridge University Press.

Alston W P (1971) Comments on Kohlberg's 'From is to ought' in: T Mischel ed. **Cognitive development and genetic epistemology**. New York, Academic Press.

Argyle M (1969) **Social interaction**. Methuen.

Atchley R C (1977) **The social forces in later life** (2nd Edition). Belmont, CA. Wadsworth.

Bahr S (1973) Effects of power and division of labor in the family in: L Hoffman & G Nye eds. **Working mothers.** San Francisco, Jossey-Bass.

Bandura A (1977) **Social learning theory**. Englewood-Cliffs NJ. Prentice-Hall.

Bandura A & F J MacDonald (1963) Influence of social reinforcement and the behaviour of models in shaping children's moral judgements. **Journal of Abnormal and Social Psychology** 67, 274-81.

Bandura A, D Ross & S Ross (1963) Imitation of film mediated aggressive models. **Journal of Abnormal and Social Psychology** 66, 3-11.

Bannister D & J Agnew (1977) The child's construing of self in: A W Landfield ed. **Nebraska symposium on motivation 1976**. University of Nebraska Press.

129

Belsky J (1979) Mother-father-infant interaction: a naturalistic observational study. **Developmental Psychology** 15, 601-7.

Belsky J G B Spanier & M Rovine (1983) Stability and change in marriage across the transition to parenthood. **Journal of Marriage and the Family** 45, 553-66.

Bem S L (1974) The measurement of psychological androgyny. **Journal of Consulting and Clinical Psychology** 42, 155-62.

Bem S L (1975) Sex-role adaptability: one consequence of psychological androgyny. **Journal of Personality and Social Psychology** 31, 634-43.

Bem S L (1983) Gender schema theory and its implications for child development: raising gender aschematic children in a gender-schematic society. **Signs** 8, 598-616.

Benedek T (1959) Parenthood as a developmental phase. **American Psychoanalytic Association Journal**, 7, 389-417.

Bernard J (1972) **The future of marriage**. New York, World.

Berndt T J (1982) The features and effects of friendships in early adolescence. **Child development**, 53, 1447-60.

Bloom K (1979) Evaluation of infant vocal conditioning. **Journal of Experimental Child Psychology** 27, 60-70.

Booth A (1977) Wife's employment and husband stress: a replication and refutation. **Journal of Marriage and the Family**, 39, 645-50.

Bowlby J (1951) **Maternal care and mental health**. Geneva, WHO.

Bowlby J (1969) **Attachment and loss: I attachment**. Hogarth Press.

Bowlby J (1980) Grief and mourning in infancy and early childhood. **Psychoanalytic Study of the Child** 15, 9-52.

Brodzinsky D, A Gormly & S Amron (1986) **Lifespan human development** (3rd Edition). HRW International Editions.

Brown G W, T O Harris & J Peto (1973) Life events and psychiatric disorders. Part 2. Nature of causal link. **Psychological Medicine**.

Bruner J S (1964) The course of cognitive growth. American Psychoanalytic Association Journal 19, 1-15.

Bruner J S, A Jolly & K Sylva (1976) **Play: its role in development and evolution**. Harmondsworth, Penguin.

Bryant P (1982) Piaget: issues and experiments. **British Journal of Psychology**. Special issue.

Bryant P E (1974) **Perception and understanding in young children**. Methuen.

Case R (1978) Intellectual development from birth to adulthood: a neo-Piagetian interpretation in: R Sielger *ed.* **Children's thinking: what develops?** Hillsdale, NJ. Erlbaum.

Cazden C (1965) **Environmental assistance to the child's acquisition of grammar**. Unpublished doctoral dissertation, Harvard University.

Chomsky N (1968) **Language and mind**. New York, Harcourt Brace.

Clark A M & A D B Clark (1976) **Early experience: myth and evidence**. Open Books.

Clausen J A (1975) The social meaning of differential physical and sexual maturation in: S E Dragastin & G H Elder, Jr. *eds.* **Adolescence in the life cycle**. New York Halsted.

Clayton P J, H A Halikes & W L Maurice (1971) Bereavement of the widowed. **Diseases of the Nervous System** 32, 597-604.

Clayton V & J E Birren (1980) Age and wisdom across the lifespan: theoretical perspectives in: P B Baltes & O G Brim, Jr. *eds.* **Lifespan development and behaviour** (Vol.1). New York, Academic Press.

Coleman J S with the assistance of J W C Johnston & K Jonassohn (1961) **The adolescent society: the social life of the teenager and its impact on education**. New York, Free Press.

Conger J J (1977) **Adolescence and youth**. New York, Harper & Row.

Conger J J & W C Miller (1966) **Personality, social class and delinquency**. New York, Wiley.

Conger J J & A Petersen (1984) **Adolescence and youth: psychological development in a changing world** (3rd edition). Harper & Row.

Cooley C H (1902) **Human nature and the social order**. New York, Scribner.

Coopersmith S (1968) Studies in self-esteem. **Scientific American**. February issue.

Cumming E & W Henry (1961) **Growing old: a process of disengagement**. New York, Basic Books.

Damon W (1977) **The social world of the child**. San Francisco, Jossey-Bass.

Dinnerstein D (1976) **The mermaid and the minotaur: sexual arrangements and human malaise**. New York, Harper & Row.

Dodd B (1972) Effects of social and vocal stimulation on infant babbling. **Developmental Psychology** 7, 80-3.

Dohrenwend B, L Krasnoff, A Askenasy & B Dohrenwend (1978) Exemplication of a method for scaling life events. **Journal of Health and Social Behaviour**, 19, 205-29.

Donaldson M (1978) **Children's minds**. Fontana.

Duberman L (1973) Step-kin relationships. **Journal of Marriage and the Family**, 35, 283-92.

Dusek J B & J F Flaherty (1981) The development of the self-concept during the adolescent years. **Monographs of the Society for Research in Child Development**, 46(Serial No 191).

Dweck C S & C I Diener (1980) An analysis of learned helplessness: II the processing of success. **Journal of Personality and Social Psychology** 39, 940-52.

Eisenberg N & R Lennon (1983) Sex differences in empathy and related capacities. **Psychological Bulletin**, 94, 100-31.

Elder G H Jr. (1980) **Family structure and socialization**. New York, Arno Press.

Entine A D (1976) Midlife counselling: prognosis and potential. **The Personnel and Guidance Journal**, 55(3), 112-4.

Erikson E H (1963) **Childhood and society**. New York, Norton.

Erikson E H (1968) **Identity: youth and crisis**. New York, Norton.

Erikson E H (1970) Reflections on the dissent of contemporary youth. **International Journal of Psychoanalysis**, 51, 11-22.

Eysenck H & G D Wilson (1973) **The experimental study of Freudian theories**. Methuen.

Fagot B I (1978) The influence of sex of child on parental reactions to toddler children. **Child Development**, 49, 459-65.

Fontana D (1981) **Psychology for teachers**. British Psychological Society.

Fox N (1977) Attachment of Kibbutz infants to mother and metapelet. **Child Development**, 48, 1228-39.

Freeman D (1984) **Margaret Mead and Samoa: the making and unmaking of the paradise island myth**. Penguin.

Freud A (1958) Adolescence in: R S Eissler, A Freud, H Hartman & M Kris *eds.* **Psychoanalytic Study of the Child**, Vol 13. New York, International Universities Press.

Freud A & S Dann (1951) An experiment in group upbringing. **The Psychoanalytic Study of the Child**, Vol VI.

Friedman S M (1952) An empirical study of the castration and Oedipus complexes. **Genetic and Psychology Monograph**, 46, 61 130.

Gardner H (1982) **Developmental psychology**. Boston, Little, Brown & Co.

Gardner A R & B Gardner (1969) Teaching sign language to a chimpanzee. **Science**, 165, 664-72.

Goffman E (1971) **The presentation of self in everyday life**. Penguin.

Goldfarb W (1943) The effects of early institutional care on adolescent personality. **Journal of Experimental Education**, 12, 106-29.

Haan N (1981) Common dimensions of personality development: early adolescence to middle life in: D Eichorn, J Clausen, N Haan, M Honzik & P Mussen *eds.* **Present and past in middle life**. New York, Academic Press.

Harlow H F (1958) The nature of love. **American Psychologist**, 13, 637-85.

Harter S (1982) **The perceived competence scale for children.** University of Denver.

Hartup W W (1983) Peer relations in: E M Hetherington *ed.* **Handbook of child psychology** Vol IV: Socialization, personality and social development. New York, Wiley.

Herriot P (1970) **An introduction to the psychology of language.** Methuen.

Hines M (1982) Prenatal gonadal hormones and sex differences in human behaviour. **Psychological Bulletin**, 92, 56-80.

Hoffman M L (1977) Moral internalisation: current theory and research in: L Berkowitz *ed.* **Advances in experimental social psychology** Vol 10. New York, Academic Press.

Hoffman M L (1979) Identification and imitation in children. **ERIC Reports E D 175 537.**

Hoffman M L (1984) Moral development in: M H Bornstein & M H Lamb *eds.* **Developmental psychology: an advanced textbook.** Hillsdale, NJ, Erlbaum.

Holmes T H & R H Rahe (1967) The social readjustment rating scale. **Journal of Psychosomatic Research**, 11, 213-8.

Horn J L & G Donaldson (1980) Cognitive development in adulthood in: O G Brim,Jr. & J Kagan *eds.* **Constancy and change in human development**. Cambridge, Mass. Harvard University Press.

Huesmann L R (1982) Television violence and agressive behaviour in: D Pearl, L Bouthilet & J Lazar *eds.* **Television and behaviour. Ten years of scientific progress and implications for the eighties**. Washington DC, US Government Printing Office.

Hughes M (1975) **Egocentrism in pre-school children**. Edinburgh University: unpublished doctoral dissertation.

Huston A C (1983) Sex-typing in: E M Hetherington *ed.* Social development. in P H Mussen (General Editor) **Carmichael's manual of child psychology** (4th edition). New York, Wiley.

Hutt C (1966) Exploration and play in children. **Symposia of the Zoological Society of London**, 18, 61-81.

Kagan J, R E Klein, G E Kinley, B Rogoff & E Nolan (1979) A cross-cultural study of cognitive development. **Monographs of the Society for Research in Child Development**, 44(5).

Kandel D B (1978) Similarity in real-life adolescent friendship pairs. **Journal of Personality and Social Psychology**, 36, 306-12.

Kavanagh R E (1974) **Facing death**. Baltimore, Penguin.

Keating D P (1980) Thinking processes in adolescence in: J Adelson ed. **Handbook of adolescent psychology**. New York, Wiley.

Kelly J B (1982) Divorce: the adult perspective in: B Wolman ed. **Handbook of developmental psychology. Englewood Cliffs, NJ. Prentice- Hall.**

Kline P (1966) Obsessional traits, obsessional symptoms and anal eroticism. **British Journal of Medical Psychology**, 41, 299-305.

Kline P (1984) **Psychology and Freudian theory: an introduction.** Methuen.

Kohlberg L (1966) A cognitive-develomental analysis of children's sex-role concepts and attitudes in: E E Maccoby ed. **The development of sex differences**. California, Stanford University Press.

Kohlberg L (1969) The cognitive-developmental approach in: D A Goslin ed. **Handbook of socialization theory and research**. Chicago, Rand McNally.

Kohlberg L (1976) Moral stages and moralisation in: T Linkons ed. **Moral development and behaviour**. New York, Holt, Rinehart & Winston. CBS College Publishing.

Kubler-Ross E (1969) **On death and dying**. New York, Macmillan.

Kuhn H H (1960) Self attitudes by age, sex and professional training. **Social Quarterly**, 1,39-55.

Langer J (1975) Interactional aspects of cognitive organisation. **Cognition**, 3, 9-28.

Lenneberg E (1967) **Biological foundations of language**. New York, Wiley

Levinger G & J Clark (1961) Emotional factors in the forgetting of work associations. **Journal of Abnormal Psychology**, 62, 99-105.

Levinson D, C Darrow, E Klein, M Levinson & B McKee (1977) Periods in the adult development of men: ages 18 to 45
in: A G Sargent *ed*. **Beyond the sex roles**. New York, West.

Lewis M & J Brooks (1975) Infants' reaction to people
in: M Lewis & L Rosenblum *eds*. **The origins of fear**. New York, Wiley.

Lowenthal M F, M Thurnher & D Chiriboga (1975) **Four stages of life: a comparative study of women and men facing transitions**. San Francisco, Jossey-Bass.

Maccoby E E & C N Jacklin (1974) **The psychology of sex differences**. Stanford, California, Stanford University Press.

Markman E M, B Cox and S Machida (1981) The standard object sorting task as a measure of conceptual organisation. **Developmental Psychology**, 17, 115-7.

Marquis D P (1931) Can conditioned responses be established in the newborn infant? **Journal of Genetic Psychology**, 39, 479-92.

Masterson J F (1967) **The psychiatric dilemma of adolescence**. Boston, Little, Brown.

McClelland D C (1955) **Studies in motivation**. New York, Appleton-Century-Crofts.

McClelland K (1982) **An exploration of the functions of friends and best friends**. Unpublished doctoral dissertation. New Jersey, Rutgers University.

McNeill D (1966) Developmental linguistics
in: F Smith & G Miller *eds*. **The genesis of language**.
    Cambridge, Mass. MIT Press.

Mead G H (1934) **Mind, self and society**. University of Chicago Press.

Mead M (1935) **Sex and temperament in three primitive societies**. New York, Morrow.

Mead M (1939) **From the South Seas: studies of adolescence and sex in primitive societies**. New York, Morrow.

Milgram S (1974) **Obedience to authority**. New York, Harper & Row.

Money J & A A Erhardt (1972) **Man & woman: boy & girl**. Baltimore, John Hopkins University Press.

Moran J J & A F Joniak (1979) Effect of language on preference for response to a moral dilemma. **Development Psychology**, 337-8.

Murray H A & C Morgan (1943) **Thematic apperception test**. Cambridge, Mass. Harvard University Press.

National Academy of Sciences, Institutes on Medicine (1984) **Bereavement, reaction, consequences and care**. Washington DC.

Neimark E D (1975) Intellectual development during adolescence in: F D Horowitz ed. **Review of child development research** Vol 4. University of Chicago Press.

Neugarten B L (1973) Personality change in late life: a developmental perspective in: C Eisdorfter & M P Lawton eds. **Psychology of adult development and aging**. Washington, DC. American Psychological Association.

Neugarten B L (1977) Personality and aging in: J E Birren & K W Schaie eds. **Handbook of the psychology of aging**. New York, Van Nostrand Rienhold.

Novak M A & H F Harlow (1975) Social recovery of monkeys isolated for the first years of life. I : Rehabilitation and therapy. **Developmental Psychology**, 11, 453-65.

Offer D (1969) **The psychological world of the teenager: a study of normal adolescence**. New York, Basic Books.

Parkin A J, J Lewinsohn & S Folkard (1982) The influence of emotion on immediate and delayed retention: Levinger and Clark reconsidered. **British Journal of Psychology**, 73, 389-93.

Parsons J E (1982) Expectancies, values and academic behaviours in: J T Spence ed. **Perspectives on achievement and achievement motivation**. San Francisco, Freeman.

Pavlov I P (1927) **Conditioned reflexes**. Oxford University Press.

Peck R (1968) Psychological development in the second half of life in: B L Neugarten ed. **Middle age and aging**. Chicago, University of Chicago Press.

Premack A J & D Premack (1972) Teaching language to an ape. **Scientific American** 222 (4), 92-9.

Reichard S, F Livson & P G Peterson (1962) **Aging and personality**. New York, Wiley.

Reiss I L (1980) **Family systems in America** (3rd edition). New York, Holt, Rinehart & Winston.

Rest J R (1983) Morality in: J Flavell & E Markman *eds. Cognitive development in P Mussen (General Editor)* **Carmichael's manual of child psychology** (4th edition) New York, Wiley.

Rheingold H, J L Gewirtz and H W Ross (1959) Social conditioning of vocalization in the infant. **Journal of Comparative and Psychological Psychology** 52, 68-73.

Robinson W P (1981) Language development in young children in: D Fontana **Psychology for teachers.**
The British Psychological Society.

Rosen B C & R d'Andrade (1959) The psychological origins of achievement motivation. **Sociometry** 22, 185-218.

Rubin Z (1980) **Children's friendships**. Cambridge, Mass, Harvard University Press.

Rubin J S, F J Provenzano & Z Luria (1974) The eye of the beholder: parents' view on sex of newborns. **American Journal of Orthopsychiatry**, 5, 353-63.

Ruble T L (1983) Sex stereotypes: issues of change in the 1970s. **Sex roles**, 9, 397-402.

Rutter M (1972) **Maternal deprivation reassessed**. Harmondsworth, Penguin.

Rutter M (1980) **Changing youth in a changing society: patterns of adolescent disorder**. Cambridge, Mass. Harvard University Press.

Rutter M, J Tizard & K Whitmore *eds. (1970)* **Education health and behaviour**. Longmans.

Schaffer H R (1977) **Mothering**. Fontana/Open Books.

Schaffer H R & P E Emerson (1964) The development of social attachments in infancy. **Monographs of social research in child development**, 29, No.94.

Schulz N R, D B Kaye & W J Hoyer (1980) Intelligence and spontaneous flexibility in adulthood and old age. **Intelligence**, 4, 219-31.

Schulz D A (1972) **The changing family: its function and future**. Englewood Cliffs, NJ. Prentice-Hall.

Schulz R (1978) **The psychology of death, dying and bereavement**. New York, Addison-Wesley.

Seligman M E P & S F Maier (1967) Failure to escape traumatic shock. **Journal of Experimental Psychology**, 74, 1-9.

Sheehy G (1976) **Passages: preditable crises of adult life**. New York, E P Dutton.

Skinner B F (1957) **Verbal behaviour**. Appleton-Century-Crofts.

Smith C & B Lloyd (1978) Maternal behaviour and perceived sex of infant: revisited. **Child Development** 49, 1263-5.

Sorensen R (1973) **Adolescent sexuality in contemporary America**. New York, William Collins.

Stephens W N (1962) **The Oedipus complex hypothesis: cross-cultural evidence**. Glencoe Ill. Free Press.

Streib G F & C Schneider (1971) **Retirement in American society**. Ithaca, NY. Cornell University Press.

Sylva K D, C Roy & M Painter (1980) **Childwatching at playgroup and nursery school**. Grant McIntyre.

Tesch S A (1983) Review of friendship development across the life span. **Human development**, 26, 266-76.

Theorell T & R H Rahe (1974) Psychosocial factors and myocardial infarction. I: an inpatient study in Sweden. **Journal of Psychosomatic Research**, 15, 25-31.

Thorndike E L (1913) **Educational psychology**. New York, Columbia University Press.

Tizard, B & J Hodges (1978) The effect of early institutional rearing on the development of eight year old children. **Journal of Child Psychology and Psychiatry**, 12, 99-118.

Trevarthen C (1974) Conversations with a two-month-old. **New Scientist**, 62, 320-3.

Troll LE (1982) **Continuations: adult development and aging.** Monterey, CA. Brooks/Cole.

Veroff J & S Feld (1970) **Marriage and work in America: a study of motives and roles.** New York, Van Nostrad Reinhold.

Vincent C E (1964) Socialization data in research on young marrieds. **Acta Sociologica**. August.

Vygotsky L (1967) Play and the role of mental development in the child. **Soviet Psychology**, 5, 6-18.

Walker K (1970) Time spent by husbands in household work. **Family Economics Review**, 14, 8-11.

Watson J B & R Rayner (1920) Conditioned emotional reactions. **Journal of Experimental Psychology** 3, 1-14.

Weiner B *ed.* (1974) **Achievement motivation and attribution theory.** Morristown, NJ, General Learning Press.

White R (1975) **Lives in progress** (3rd edition). New York, Holt, Rinehart & Winston.

Wiseman R (1975) Crisis theory and the process of divorce. **Social casework**, 56,205-12.

Yarrow L (1973) The relationship between nutritive sucking experiences in infancy and non-nutritive sucking in childhood
in: H J Eysenck & G D Wilson eds. **The experimental study of Freudian theories.** Methuen.

Index